11+ Maths

For the **CEM** test

These 10-Minute Tests from CGP are perfect for short bursts of 11+ practice — just what children need to keep their skills fresh in the run-up to the test.

Each test is packed with realistic CEM-style questions, with detailed answers at the back of the book. There's even a progress chart to keep track of their scores.

This is Book 2. For more quick-fire tests at the same level, don't miss Book 1!

10-Minute Tests

Ages 10-11

--- **How to access your free Online Edition** ---

This book includes a free Online Edition to read on your PC, Mac or tablet.
You'll just need to go to **cgpbooks.co.uk/extras** and enter this code:

0224 1068 3831 0607

By the way, this code only works for one person. If somebody else has used this book before you, they might have already claimed the Online Edition.

How to use this book

This book is made up of 10-minute tests and puzzle pages.
There are answers and detailed explanations in the pull-out section at the back of the book.

10-Minute Tests

- There are 31 tests in this book, each containing 12 questions.

- Each test is designed to cover a good range of the question styles and topics that your child could come across in the maths section of their 11+ test, at the same difficulty level.

- Your child should aim to score around 10 or 11 out of 12 in each 10-minute test.
  If they score less than this, use their results to work out the areas they need more practice on.

- If your child hasn't managed to finish the test in time, they need to work on increasing their speed, whereas if they have made a lot of mistakes, they need to work more carefully.

- Keep track of your child's scores using the progress chart on the inside back cover of the book.

Puzzle Pages

- There are 6 puzzle pages in this book, which are a great break from test-style questions. They encourage children to practise the same skills that they will need in the test, but in a fun way.

Published by CGP

Editors:
Emily Forsberg, Sharon Keeley-Holden, Dawn Wright

With thanks to Alison Griffin and Andy Park for the proofreading.

Please note that CGP is not associated with CEM in any way.
This book does not include any official questions and it is not endorsed by CEM.

ISBN: 978 1 78908 180 0
Printed by Elanders Ltd, Newcastle upon Tyne
Clipart from Corel®

Based on the classic CGP style created by Richard Parsons.

Text, design, layout and original illustrations © Coordination Group Publications Ltd. (CGP) 2018
All rights reserved.

Photocopying this book is not permitted, even if you have a CLA licence.
Extra copies are available from CGP with next day delivery. • 0800 1712 712 • www.cgpbooks.co.uk

Contents

Test 1 2
Test 2 5
Test 3 8
Test 4 11
Test 5 14

Puzzles 1 17

Test 6 18
Test 7 21
Test 8 24
Test 9 27
Test 10 30

Puzzles 2 33

Test 11 34
Test 12 37
Test 13 40
Test 14 43
Test 15 46

Puzzles 3 49

Test 16 50
Test 17 53
Test 18 56
Test 19 59
Test 20 62

Puzzles 4 65

Test 21 66
Test 22 69
Test 23 72
Test 24 75
Test 25 78

Puzzles 5 81

Test 26 82
Test 27 85
Test 28 88
Test 29 91
Test 30 94
Test 31 97

Puzzles 6 100

Test 1

You have **10 minutes** to do this test. Work as quickly and accurately as you can.

Five people took part in a long-jump competition.
The distances they jumped are recorded in the table below.

Adam	Bing	Cho	Dave	Emma
4.35 m	3.97 m	4.32 m	4.20 m	4.02 m

1. Who jumped the second longest distance? Circle the correct option.

    A   Adam   C   Cho   E   Emma
    B   Bing   D   Dave

2. Give the distance Emma jumped in millimetres.

   ▢▢▢▢▢ mm

3. A regular pentagon is cut along the dotted line shown.
   Two identical new shapes are produced.

   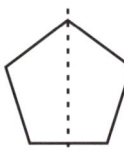

   How many obtuse angles are there in one of the new shapes?

   ▢

4. Kailash has £43.90. He then gets paid £27.63 and wins £75 in a poetry competition. How much money does he have now?

   £▢▢▢.▢▢

5. Tina visited six different supermarkets and wrote down the price of 1 kg of pears in each one. The prices are listed below.

   97p, £1.03, £1.20, £1.25, £1, £1.15

   Calculate the mean price of 1 kg of pears.

6. There is normally 400 g of mushrooms in a pack. A special offer pack of mushrooms has 20% extra free. What is the mass of the special offer pack?

7. Film A was made in the year MCMLXXV.
   Film B was made in the year MCMLXXXIV.
   How many years after Film A was Film B made? Circle the correct option.

   A   11   C   9   E   15
   B   10   D   4

Lucas asks everyone in Year 6 where they would like to go on a trip.
He makes a pie chart of the results.

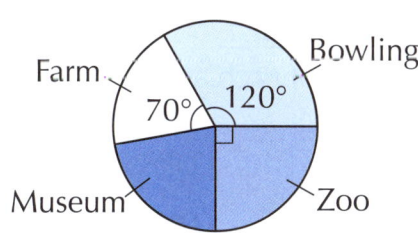

8. What fraction of the children said they wanted to go to either the farm or the zoo? Circle the correct option.

   A 2/5   B 4/9   C 5/9   D 1/3   E 2/7

9. 24 children said they wanted to go bowling.
   How many said they wanted to go to the zoo?

10. Mr Smith is knitting a scarf. It takes him 1½ minutes to knit each row. He starts knitting at 5:15 pm. At what time will he have knitted 60 rows?

☐☐:☐☐ pm

11. Points A and B are joined with a line on the coordinate grid below.

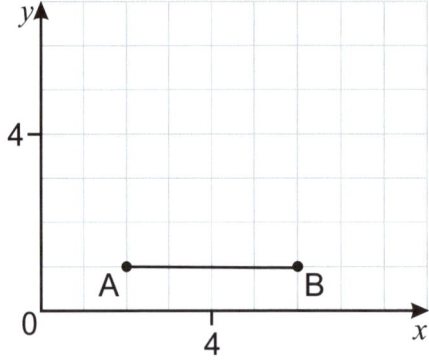

☐ = 1 cm²

Point C is added to the grid at (5, 4). It is joined to points A and B. What is the area of the triangle formed?

☐☐ cm²

12. The diagram below shows a quadrilateral. An expression is given for the size of each angle in degrees.

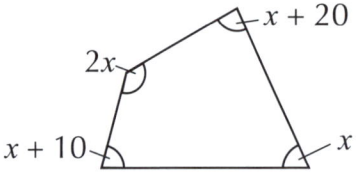

not drawn accurately

Which equation is correct? Circle the correct option.

A $3x + 30x = 360$
B $35x = 360$
C $5x = 180$
D $5x = 330$
E $5x = 390$

/ 12

Test 2

You have **10 minutes** to do this test. Work as quickly and accurately as you can.

1. John creates a sequence by counting back in steps of 4.
   The first term in his sequence is 100. What will the third term be?

2. Bananas cost 13p each. Chris buys five bananas and pays with a £5 note.
   How much change does he get?

3. What is 56 855 rounded to the nearest 100?

4. Which of the shapes below has exactly one line of symmetry?
   Circle the correct option.

   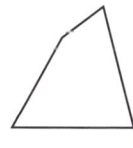   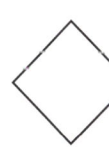   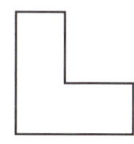   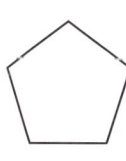

      A   B   C   D   E

5. | 204 × 7001 = 1 428 204 |

   What is 2040 × 7.001? Circle the correct option.
   - A   14.28204
   - B   142.8204
   - C   1428.204
   - D   14 282.04
   - E   142 820.4

Max and Holly attend a holiday club. The percentage of time that they each spend on the different types of activity is shown on the chart below.

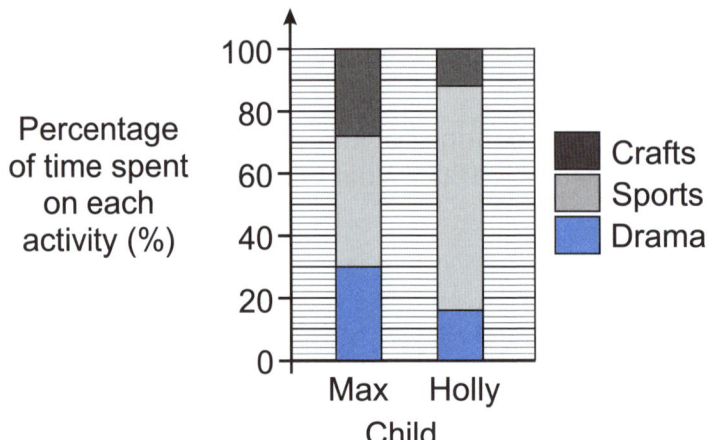

6. What percentage of Holly's time was spent doing sports? Circle the correct option.

    A   30%
    B   72%
    C   42%
    D   66%
    E   88%

7. The children spend 2½ hours at the holiday club.
    How long, in minutes, did Max spend doing drama?

     mins

Aneena is making a path across her garden using square slabs.
The path is one slab wide. This diagram shows the first three slabs she lays.

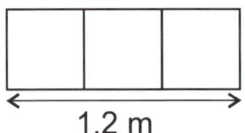

8. What is the area of one slab? Give your answer in cm².

     cm²

9. The path needs to be 24 m long. How many slabs are needed?

10. A block of ice cream is shown in the diagram below.

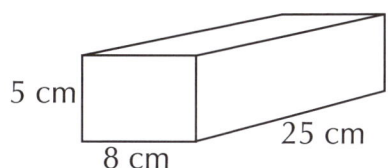

Mohammed ate $1/4$ of the block of ice cream.
What volume of ice cream did he eat?

 cm³

11. Find the size of angle a, shown in the diagram below.

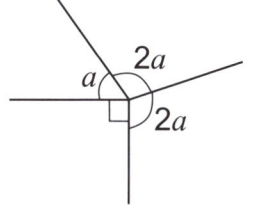   not drawn accurately

 °

12. Henry has written an expression. When $x = 4$, the value of the expression is 24.
Which of the following could not have been Henry's expression?
Circle the correct option.

    A $x(x + 2)$
    B $1/2(x + 11x)$
    C $4x + 8$
    D $8(x - 1)$
    E $5x + 5$

/ 12

Test 3

You have **10 minutes** to do this test. Work as quickly and accurately as you can.

1. Which of the shapes below is a regular quadrilateral?
   Circle the correct option.

   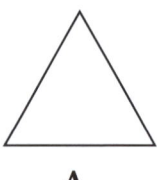  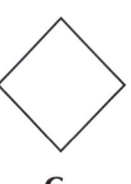 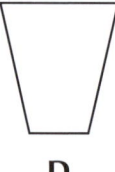 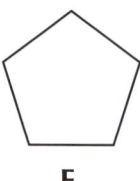

   A   B   C   D   E

2. Mike planted some sunflower seeds on April 29th.
   The shoots appeared on May 4th.
   How many days after planting did the shoots appear?

    days

3. The graph below shows the changing temperature in a greenhouse one day.

   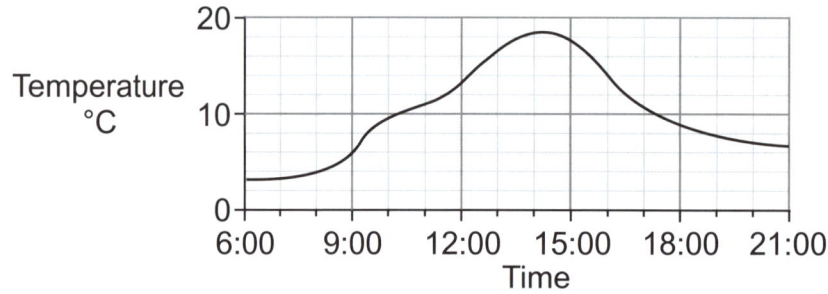

   Use the graph to find the approximate temperature in the greenhouse at half past three in the afternoon. Circle the correct option.

        A   12 °C
        B   13 °C
        C   14 °C
        D   16 °C
        E   18 °C

Red pens come in packs of 12 and blue pens come in packs of 20.

4. What is the ratio of red pens in a pack to blue pens in a pack?
Give your answer in its simplest form.

5. A teacher orders 40 packs of red pens and 9 packs of blue pens.
How many pens have been ordered in total?

This pictogram shows the number of football cards owned by four children.

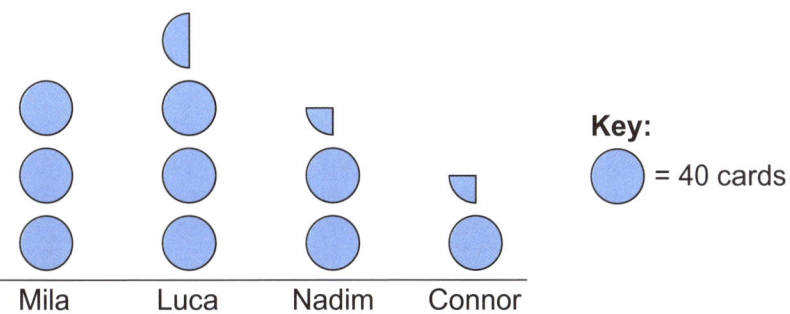

6. Mila gives Nadim some of her cards so that they both have the same number.
How many cards does Mila have now?

7. What is the mean number of cards owned by the four children?

8. This formula can be used to convert a distance in miles, m, to kilometres, k.

$$k = 8m \div 5$$

Using this formula, convert 20 miles to kilometres.

km

9. Which of the following is not equivalent to the others? Circle the correct option.

   A   ³⁄₁₀ of 60
   B   10% of 180
   C   ³⁄₄ of 24
   D   0.18 × 1000
   E   5% of 360

10. Linda has 5860 ml of pancake batter. She uses 45 ml of batter to make each pancake. She makes as many pancakes of this size as she can. How much batter is left over?

The diagram shows the line AB. Line CD is parallel to AB.
Line CD is half as long as line AB.

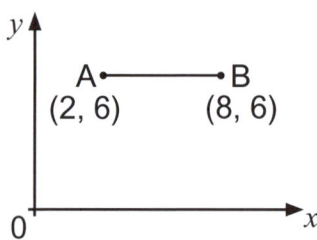

11. Which of these could be the coordinates of C and D? Circle the correct option.

   A   C(3, 4) and D(3, 7)   D   C(4, 4) and D(8, 8)
   B   C(2, 4) and D(5, 4)   E   C(3, 4) and D(6, 1)
   C   C(1, 4) and D(7, 4)

12. Line AB is reflected in the x-axis, then translated 1 unit left. What are the new coordinates of A? Circle the correct option.

   A   (2, −5)   C   (−2, 5)   E   (−1, −6)
   B   (1, −6)   D   (−3, 6)

/ 12

Test 4

You have **10 minutes** to do this test. Work as quickly and accurately as you can.

1. Mr Jones puts seven tulips on each table in his restaurant. He has three left over. How many tulips could there be in total? Circle the correct option.

   A 60   C 56   E 11
   B 21   D 59

2. It is −18 °C inside a freezer. Its door is left open and the temperature inside increases by 5 °C. What is the temperature in the freezer now?

    °C

3. The net below is folded to make a 3D shape.

   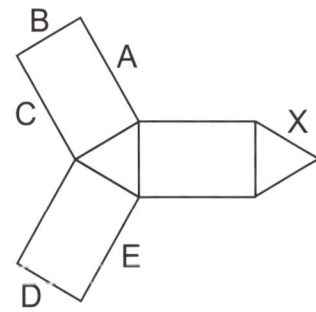

   Which side of the net joins to side X? Circle the correct option.

   A   B   C   D   E

4. A ball is dropped onto the ground. The heights of its bounces form a sequence. The heights of its first four bounces are shown in the table below.

Bounce 1	Bounce 2	Bounce 3	Bounce 4
40 cm	20 cm	10 cm	5 cm

   What will be the height of its sixth bounce?

   ⬜⬜.⬜⬜ cm

40 children at a playgroup are given a biscuit and a drink. The children each chose between a chocolate biscuit and a plain biscuit and between juice and milk. The table below shows the number of children who chose each option.

	Juice	Milk	Total
Chocolate		5	9
Plain			
Total	12		40

5. How many children chose a plain biscuit and juice?

6. What percentage of the children chose juice?

 %

7. Work out the area of the shape below.

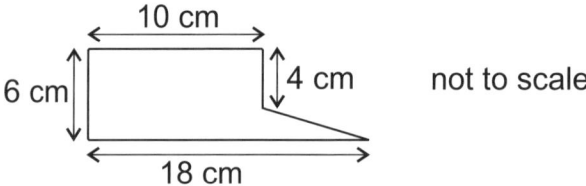

not to scale

 cm²

8. Noah fills 26 empty jars with homemade jam. An empty jar has a mass of 95 g. Noah puts 450 g of jam into each jar. What is the total mass of the filled jam jars?

 g

9. Work out $^2/_5 + ^2/_3$. Circle the correct option.

    A $^4/_{15}$ C $1^2/_{15}$ E $2^2/_5$

    B $^4/_5$ D $1^1/_{15}$

10. What is the size of angle *b* in the diagram below?

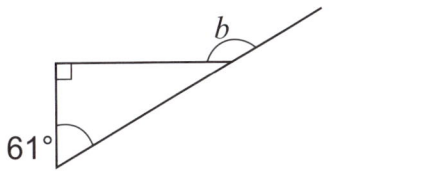

☐☐☐°

It costs £6 to enter Smashers Pottery Studio. You then pay £3.25 for each plate you paint.

11. Circle the expression that shows the total cost, in pounds, of painting *p* plates.

    A   9.25*p*
    B   6(3.25*p*)
    C   6 + 3.25*p*
    D   6*p* + 3.25
    E   6 – 3.25*p*

12. The graph below shows the cost of painting plates at Plates R Us Pottery Studio. Plates R Us is free to enter.

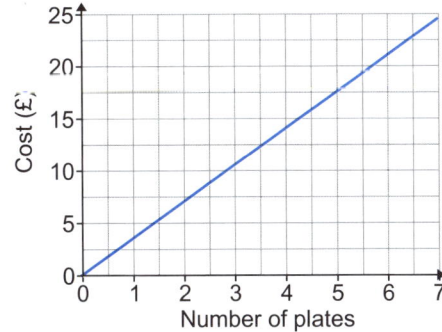

Gina wants to paint ten plates.
How much will she save by going to Plates R Us instead of Smashers?

£

Test 5

You have **10 minutes** to do this test. Work as quickly and accurately as you can.

1. A regular pentagon has a perimeter of 600 mm. How long is each side?

    mm

2. What is 148 979 − 20 072.2?
   Use estimation, then circle the exact answer from these options.

   A   139 456.8
   B   28 029.7
   C   168 906.8
   D   128 906.8
   E   60 610.7

3. The diameter of a circle is 12.8 cm. What is the radius of the circle?

    cm

4. Ash has a 7 m wide wall in his bedroom. Ash works out that he can fit four different items from those shown below across the wall with no space left over.

   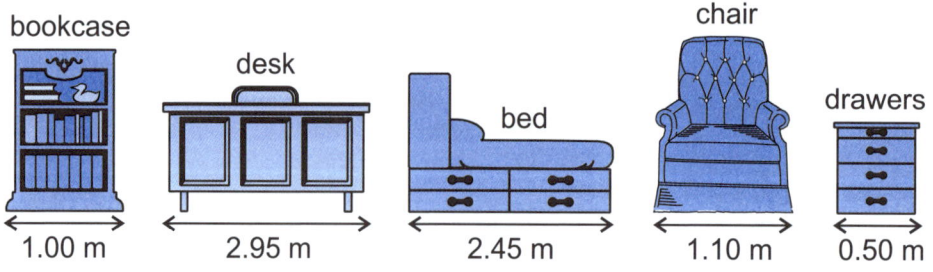

   Which item does Ash not use? Circle the correct option.

   A   bookcase   C   bed   E   drawers
   B   desk   D   chair

5. Ruby has $1/3$ of a pizza on her plate. She cuts it into three equal slices.
   What fraction of the whole pizza is each of these three pieces?
   Circle the correct option.

   A $1/9$ C $1/6$ E $1/27$
   B $2/9$ D $1/4$

6. A tent covers a rectangular area of ground measuring 4.32 m by 6 m.
   What area of ground does the tent cover?

    m²

7. This bar chart shows the number of bikes sold in different years by a bike company.

   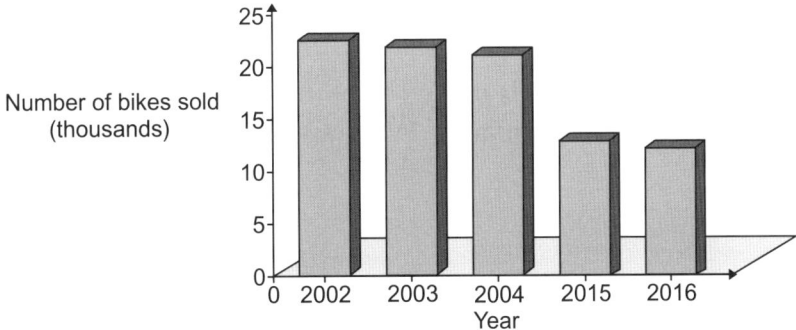

   Why is this bar chart misleading? Circle the correct option.
   A The bars should not be shown as 3D blocks.
   B The bars should be different colours.
   C Some years have been missed out.
   D There is no grid to help you read the values exactly.
   E The scale should go up in ones.

8. A candle is lit at 6:30 pm. It burns at a steady rate and lasts until 8:45 pm.
   At what time had $1/5$ of the candle burned?

   ☐ : ☐ ☐ pm

9. Sarah takes five spelling tests. Her mean mark for the five tests is 7.
She takes a sixth test. Her mean mark for the six tests is 6.
How many marks did she get in the sixth test?

10. Lucy starts at a number and counts up in steps of 8. One of the numbers she counts is 17. Which of these numbers could she have started at? Circle the correct option.

   A   −16   C   −23   E   −1
   B   −17   D   −24

11. On a coordinate grid, a coin is placed at point (−2, −1). The coin is then moved left one square and up two squares. What are the coordinates of the coin now?

12. Omar makes the patterns below out of blocks.

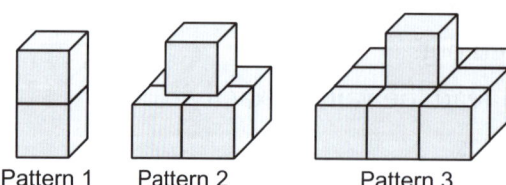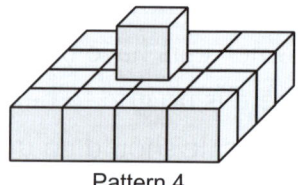

Pattern 1   Pattern 2   Pattern 3   Pattern 4

Which expression represents the number of blocks in the nth pattern in the sequence? Circle the correct option.

   A $2n + 1$ C $n^2 - 1$ E $n^2 + n$
   B $n^2 + 1$ D n^2

/ 12

Puzzles 1

Now for a break from 10-minute tests. Try out your skills on this puzzle.

Pyramid Problem

To be allowed to enter the Great Pyramid of Multiplia without being cursed, explorers must first solve a puzzle.

Each box on the pyramid must hold a number that is a multiple of all the numbers in the circles attached to it. An example mini-pyramid is shown on the right:

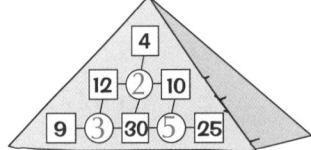

Oh, one more thing. You have to use these numbers — use each exactly once.

140   105   6   8   22   57   15   210   84   12

Test 6

You have **10 minutes** to do this test. Work as quickly and accurately as you can.

1. In which of the numbers below does the 7 have the largest value?
   Circle the correct answer.

   A 1 234 567
   B 172.8
   C 10 007
   D 952.7
   E 65 427.99

The quiz scores of four teams are shown on the pictogram below.

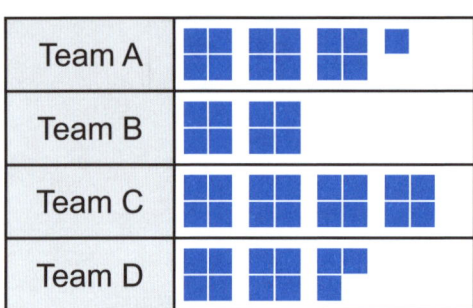

Key: = 8 points

2. How many more points did Team D get than Team B?

3. Team E got 30 points. Circle the option which shows Team E's points.

   A    C    E

   B   D

4. A rectangle has a width of 15 cm. Its length is twice its width.
   What is the perimeter of the rectangle?

   ▢▢ cm

5. A teacher asks a class to write down as many different ways as they can think of to make the number 24. Jas writes down all the statements below. Which one is wrong? Circle this statement.

    A   Square five then subtract one.
    B   Divide 144 by six.
    C   Find five percent of 120.
    D   Multiply eight by three.
    E   Subtract 76 from one hundred.

6. Lia pours out 150 ml of lemonade from a full 2.5 litre bottle. How much lemonade is left in the bottle? Circle the correct answer.

    A   1 litre
    B   2.25 litres
    C   2.485 litres
    D   2 litres
    E   2.35 litres

7. Stevie draws the triangle shown below. It has an area of 24 cm².

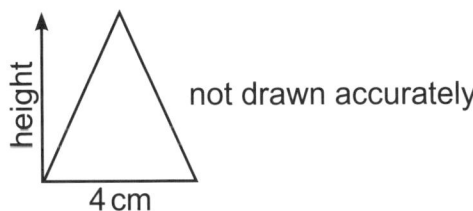

What is the height of the triangle?  cm

8. Each letter below is a Roman numeral.

I V X L C M

Find the sum of the numerals shown which have exactly one line of symmetry. Write your answer in figures.

9. Find the sum of the two prime numbers between 30 and 40.

10. Adam collects eggs every day. From Monday to Friday, Adam earns £7.00 per day. He earns double this amount per day at the weekend.
What is the mean amount he earns per day over the full week?

11. Which of the following expressions can be used to describe angle b in the diagram?
Circle the correct option.

    A $360° - a$
    B a
    C $2a$
    D $360° - 2a$
    E $180° - a$

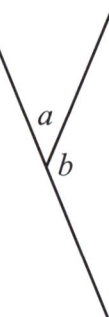

12. The cost, B, in pounds, for each person to attend a board games event can be found using the formula $B = (24 \div n) + 2.5$.
n is the number of people attending the event.
How much will it cost per person if 10 people attend?

Test 7

You have **10 minutes** to do this test. Work as quickly and accurately as you can.

1. The number 8 bus always runs exactly on time.
   Part of its timetable is shown below.

Bus Station	Cinema	City Park	High Street	Back Street
1425	1437	1455	1504	1515

   Dan is waiting at the High Street stop. It is 2:47 pm.
   How long will he have to wait for the number 8 bus?

   ☐☐ minutes

2. Which of the following rounds to 20 000?
   Circle the correct answer.

   A 2499 to the nearest 1000.
   B 19 590 to the nearest 100.
   C 19 590 to the nearest 1000.
   D 20 005 to the nearest 10.
   E 20 500 to the nearest 1000.

Jack and Jill are making 3D shapes from coloured cubes.
Each of Jack's cubes has a width of 1 cm.

3. Jack used six of his cubes to make the shape shown here. What is the area of the bottom face of the shape?

   ☐☐ cm²

4. Jill's cubes are 2 cm wide. Jill makes a shape using three of her cubes. How many cubes would Jack need to use to make the same shape?

   ☐☐

5. What is the remainder when 2576 is divided by 9?

6. Look at the number line below.

   What number is the arrow pointing to? Circle the correct answer.

   A $2\frac{2}{3}$ B $\frac{10}{3}$ C $3\frac{3}{4}$ D $\frac{13}{3}$ E 3

7. Which of the following shapes has the same area as the shape shown below?
   Circle the correct option.

   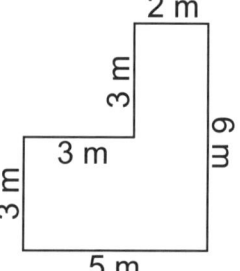

   A   A square, width 5 m
   B   A rectangle, width 4 m, length 5 m
   C   A parallelogram, base 7 m, vertical height 3 m
   D   A triangle, base 10 m, height 4 m
   E   None of the above

8. Kemi thinks of a number, divides it by 1000 then adds $\frac{1}{4}$ to get 5.
   What was the number Kemi thought of?

9. Mark says,
   "My age lies between the squares of 6 and 7.
   It is a prime number, and the digits have a difference of 1."
   How old is Mark?

10. The graph below can be used to help convert between miles and kilometres.

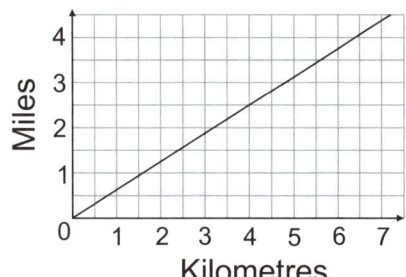

Use the graph to convert 25 miles to kilometres.

☐☐☐ km

11. The shape on the right is a kite.
Which of the following is true?
Circle the correct answer.

    A $x + y = 60°$
    B $x + y = 240°$
    C $x + y = 360°$
    D $x + y = 120°$
    E $x + y = 180°$

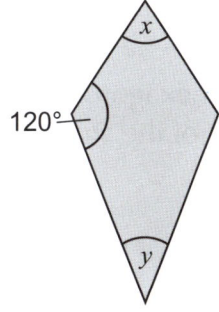

not drawn accurately

12. A number sequence starts on an even number, and its 10th term is odd.
Which of the expressions below could be the nth term of this sequence?
Circle the correct option.

    A $2n$ C n^2 E $n^2 + 1$
    B $20 - 2n$ D $2n + 1$

/ 12

Test 8

You have **10 minutes** to do this test. Work as quickly and accurately as you can.

1. A small packet of popcorn costs 80p. A multipack containing five small packets costs £3.80. How much money is saved by buying a multipack instead of five small packets?

   p

2. The shape below is made from three identical regular hexagons.

   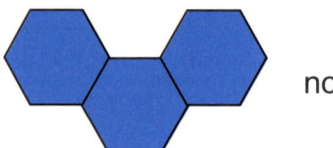 not drawn accurately

   The perimeter of one hexagon is 36 mm.
   What is the perimeter of the shape?

    mm

The shoe sizes of five people are: 7, 3, 5, 2, 4.

3. One of the following statements is not true. Circle this statement.

   A   The difference between the largest and smallest shoe sizes is 5.
   B   When written in size order, the middle number is 4.
   C   The total of the shoe sizes is a prime number.
   D   All the shoe sizes are either square or prime numbers.
   E   The largest shoe size multiplied by the smallest shoe size is 14.

4. The shoe size of a sixth person is added to the list.
   The mean shoe size of the six people is 5.
   What is the shoe size of the sixth person?

5. Jen makes a sequence of numbers using the following rule to find the next number:
   "Double the previous number and add nine."
   Which of these could be Jen's sequence? Circle the correct answer.

   A   1, 2, 9...   C   3, 15, 39...   E   1, 10, 29...
   B   1, 11, 22...   D   2, 11, 20...

6. A cross and five lines, labelled Q-U, have been drawn on the coordinate grid to the right.
   The cross is translated 5 squares up and 2 squares left. On which line does the cross now lie?
   Circle the correct option.

   A   Line Q
   B   Line R
   C   Line S
   D   Line T
   E   Line U

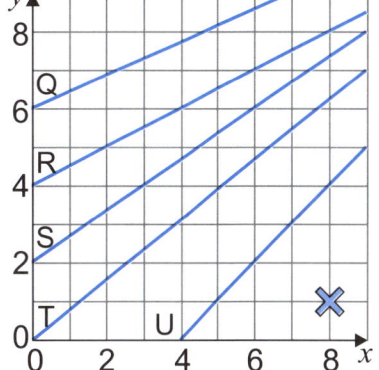

Kate ran to the top of a hill and back down again. The graph below shows how her height above the bottom of the hill changed during the run.

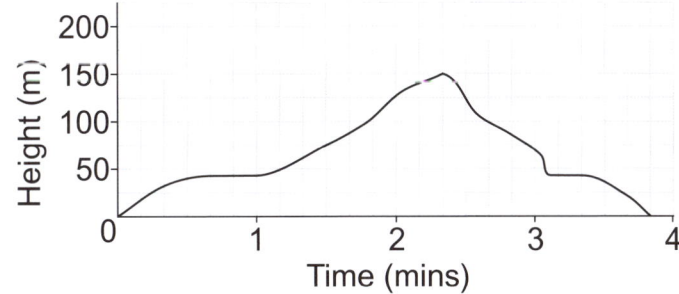

7. After how many seconds was Kate first halfway up the hill? ▢▢▢ s

8. Last time she ran down the hill, it took her 1 minute 45 seconds.
   How many seconds faster was she this time?

    seconds

Cat has two circular bracelets, as shown below. The smaller bracelet's diameter and circumference are ²/₃ of that of the larger bracelet.

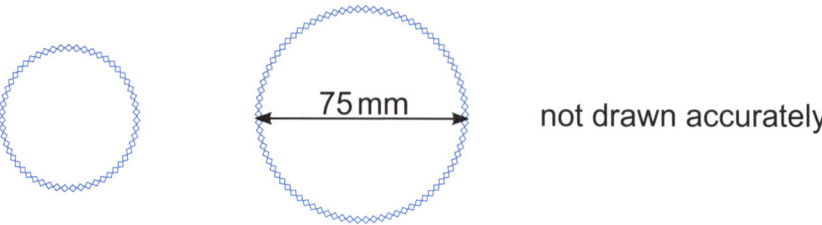

not drawn accurately

9. What is the radius of the smaller bracelet?

☐☐ mm

10. Each bracelet has a number of jewels evenly spaced around the circumference. The spacing is the same on each bracelet. There are 25 jewels in total on both bracelets. How many jewels are on the larger bracelet? Circle the correct answer.

    A 5   **B** 10   **C** 15   **D** 17   **E** 20

The ages of two sisters, Abi (aged A) and Bella (aged B) satisfy the equation $2A - 3B = 3$.

11. Which of the following could be Abi and Bella's ages?
Circle the correct option.
    A   Abi is 4, Bella is 1
    B   Abi is 3, Bella is 2
    C   Abi is 3, Bella is 3
    D   Abi is 3, Bella is 1
    E   Abi is 4, Bella is 2

12. Bella is actually 9 years old. How old is Abi?

☐☐

/ 12

Test 9

You have **10 minutes** to do this test. Work as quickly and accurately as you can.

1. What is the size of the acute angle in the diagram?

   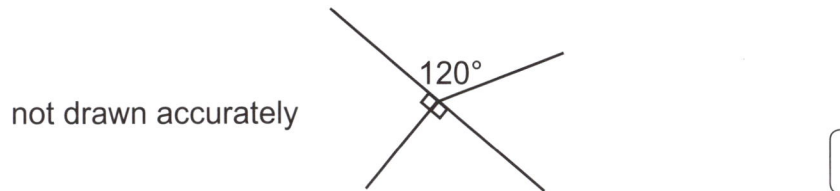

   not drawn accurately

2. Which of the following is an increase in temperature of 10 °C?
   Circle the correct option.

   A   −1 °C to 11 °C
   B   7 °C to −3 °C
   C   −5.9 °C to 6.1 °C.
   D   −5.5 °C to 4.5 °C
   E   −27 °C to −37 °C

Gita is making tea and coffee for a meeting.
The part-filled table below shows the drinks that people have requested.

	With Milk	No Milk	Total
Coffee		15	
Tea	13		29
Total			65

3. How many people wanted coffee with milk?

4. What percentage of people wanted tea with milk?
   Circle the correct option.

   A   2%   B   5%   C   10%   D   20%   E   50%

The bar chart below shows the number of people with different hair colours at a party.

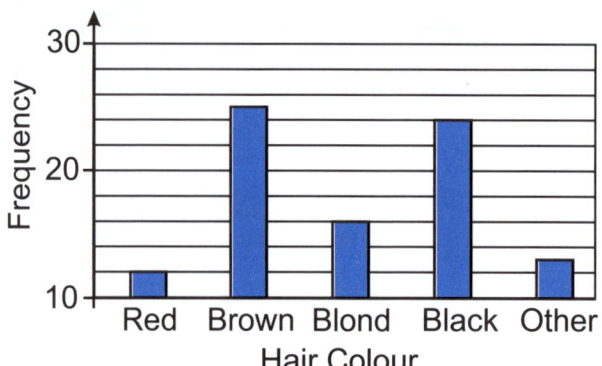

5. What hair colour is twice as common as one of the other colours? Circle the correct option.

   A Red   B Brown   C Blond   D Black   E Other

6. Why is the bar chart misleading? Circle the correct statement.
   A It doesn't allow for people with grey hair.
   B The vertical axis doesn't increase evenly.
   C The height of the bar for brown hair is not a whole number.
   D The bars should be coloured to match the hair colours.
   E The vertical axis doesn't start at zero.

Jo is following a recipe to make 18 chocolate muffins.
She measures out 450 g of caster sugar into a mixing bowl.

7. What will be the mean amount of caster sugar in each muffin?

   ☐☐ g

8. The other ingredients are added to the mixing bowl. The total mass of all the ingredients is 2.5 times the mass of just the sugar. Find the mass of the other ingredients. Give your answer in kilograms.

   ☐.☐☐☐ kg

9. $^2/_3 x = 90$. What is the value of x?

   ☐☐☐

10. What is the area of the shape below?

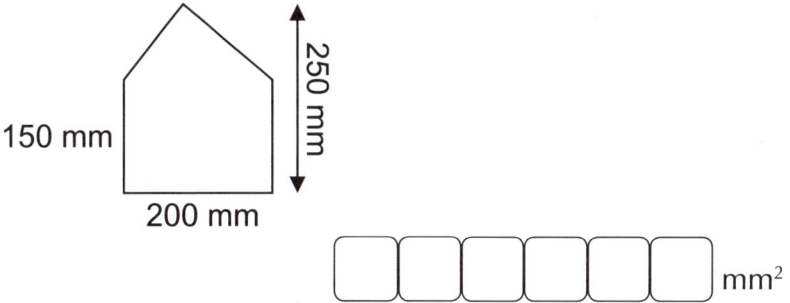

☐☐☐☐☐☐ mm²

11. Which of these is the largest proportion?
    Circle the correct answer.

    A $\frac{1}{4} \times \frac{1}{3}$
    B $\frac{1}{4} + \frac{1}{3}$
    C $\frac{2}{3} - \frac{1}{4}$
    D $\frac{1}{3} \div 4$
    E $\frac{1}{4} \times 3$

12. The first three shapes in a sequence of cubes is shown below.

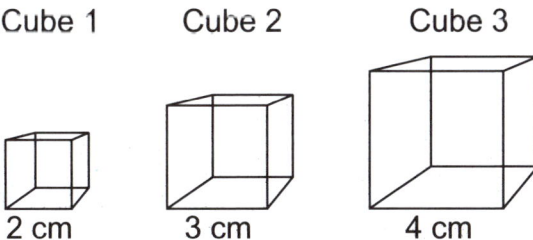

What is the volume of the 9th cube in the sequence?

 cm³

/ 12

Test 10

You have **10 minutes** to do this test. Work as quickly and accurately as you can.

1. Four irregular shapes are shown below.

   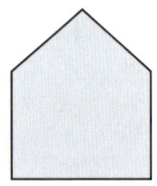  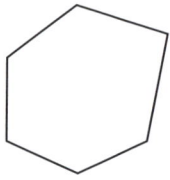 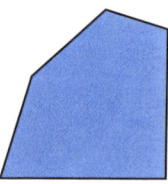

   Which of the following statements about the four shapes is correct?
   Circle the correct answer.

   - A   There are three hexagons and one pentagon.
   - B   There are four pentagons.
   - C   There are two pentagons and two hexagons.
   - D   There are three pentagons and one hexagon.
   - E   There are four hexagons.

2. What is the largest factor of 50 that is also a factor of 60?

3. Cheshire cheese is usually priced at £1.50 per 100 g. How much would 100 g of Cheshire cheese cost if the price was reduced by 10%?

4. A square has a perimeter of 44 cm. What is its area in cm²?

    cm²

5. The ruler below shows inches and centimetres.

   Use the ruler to estimate the number of inches in one metre, to the nearest 10 inches. Circle the correct option.

   A   20 inches
   B   40 inches
   C   200 inches
   D   250 inches
   E   400 inches

6. There are fewer than 200 pupils in one year group. The pupils can be split up into 9 classes, with an equal number of pupils in each class. They can also be split up into 10 classes, with an equal number of pupils in each class. What is the largest possible number of pupils in the year group?

The pie chart below shows how 200 people responded when they were asked, "Do you own a pet?" The angle for the "Yes" sector is 45°.

7. Of the people that own a pet, half own a dog.
   What fraction of the total own a dog? Circle the correct answer.

   A ½   B ¼   C ⅛   D ¹⁄₁₆   E ¹⁄₂₀

8. How many people said that they do not own a pet?

9. The diagram below shows a design made up of a circle and some rectangles.

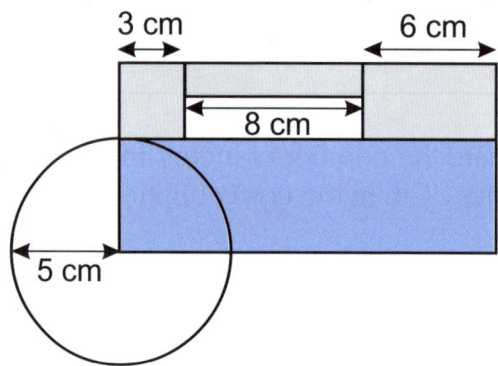

Use the diagram to find the area of the blue rectangle.

 cm²

10. The first four terms in a sequence are 1, 9, 25 and 49.
What is the next term in the sequence?

A point on a grid has coordinates $(x, 2x + 1)$.

11. Which of the points labelled on the grid below could this be?
Give the letter of the correct point.

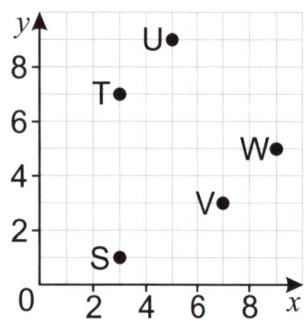

12. The point is translated two squares to the left and one square up.
Which of the following describes the coordinates of the translated point?
Circle the correct option.

A $(x + 1, 2x + 2)$ C $(x – 2, 2x – 1)$ E $(x – 2, 2x + 2)$
B $(x – 1, 2x + 3)$ D $(x + 2, 2x + 2)$

/ 12

Puzzles 2

Now for a break from 10-minute tests. Try out your skills on these puzzles.

Safe as Houses

Ms Match keeps a spare door key in an electronic safe in the shed.

It is accessed with a 5-digit code. There are no repeated digits in the code. Consecutive numbers, such as 3 and 4, or 8 and 9, are not found next to each other in the code.

If a wrong code is entered, the safe is programmed to give clues. Two attempts to input the code are shown below, with the clues given by the safe.

Can you use the clues to crack the code for the safe?

Interesting Times

All three clocks in Andy's house show different times:

Use these facts to work out the correct time:

- One clock is one minute slow.
- One clock is fifteen minutes slow.
- One clock stopped exactly eleven and a half hours ago.
- It's now afternoon.

Test 11

You have **10 minutes** to do this test. Work as quickly and accurately as you can.

1. Circle the most likely length of a netball court.

   A 30.5 km   C 30.5 cm   E 30.5 m²
   B 30.5 mm   D 30.5 m

2. What number is the arrow pointing to? Circle the correct answer.

   A 2.51   B 2.9   C 2.49   D 2.48   E 2.95

3. An ant is at point A on the coordinate grid below facing north. He turns 90° anticlockwise and walks forward two squares. Give the coordinates of the ant's new position.

   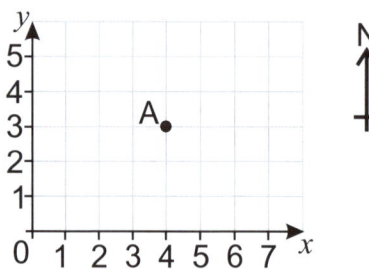

   (☐ , ☐)

4. Lisa and Marc are cycling around a circular track. They leave the start line at the same time. Lisa cycles once around the track every 2½ minutes and Marc cycles once around the track every 3 minutes. How many minutes will it be before they next leave the start line at the same time?

   ☐☐☐ minutes

In a football club there are 40 children. ¹/₅ of the children are 9 years old, 15% are 10 years old and the rest are 11 years old.

5. How many of the children are 11 years old? Circle the correct answer.

   A 6 B 14 C 20 D 26 E 30

6. The football coach wants to draw a pie chart showing the proportions of children of different ages in the club. What angle should the '9 years old' sector have? Circle the correct answer.

   A 72° B 54° C 36° D 15° E 45°

7. A 500 g bag of bird seed costs £1.99. Paul needs 4.5 kg of bird seed. How much will this cost?

   £ ☐☐.☐☐

8. The perimeter of the rectangular field shown is 44 m.

   12 m

   not drawn accurately

   What is the area of the field?

   ☐☐☐ m²

9. Tom needs 2p coins to play a game at an amusement arcade. He changes two £2 coins and three 20p coins for 2p coins. How many 2p coins does he receive?

   ☐☐☐☐

10. Jamie says, "I am thinking of two prime numbers that are both less than 20. If I add them together and double the result, I get 30."
What are the two numbers Jamie is thinking of?

 and

11. Two mothers are comparing the masses of their babies.
Baby Eric is 5.5 pounds and baby Sue is 3.5 kg.

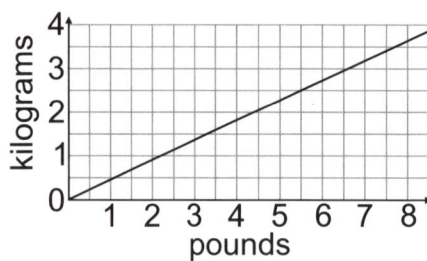

Which statement is true? Circle the correct answer.
- **A** Baby Sue is heavier than baby Eric by 2 kg.
- **B** Baby Eric is heavier than baby Sue by 1 kg.
- **C** Baby Sue is heavier than baby Eric by about 2.25 pounds.
- **D** Baby Sue is heavier than baby Eric by exactly 2 pounds.
- **E** Baby Eric is heavier than baby Sue by 2.25 pounds.

12. The circumference, C, of a circle with diameter, d, is given by this formula:
$$C = 3.14d$$

What is the circumference of a circle with a diameter of 20 cm?

 cm

Test 12

You have **10 minutes** to do this test. Work as quickly and accurately as you can.

1. What is six million, four hundred and thirty thousand and seventy-two in figures? Circle the correct answer.

    A   64 372
    B   6 430 720
    C   6 043 072
    D   6 430 072
    E   643 072

2. Ron is doing a sponsored walk. After walking 8 km, he has done 25% of the walk. How long is the walk?

     km

In a talent show, children voted for their favourite act. Here is a chart of the results.

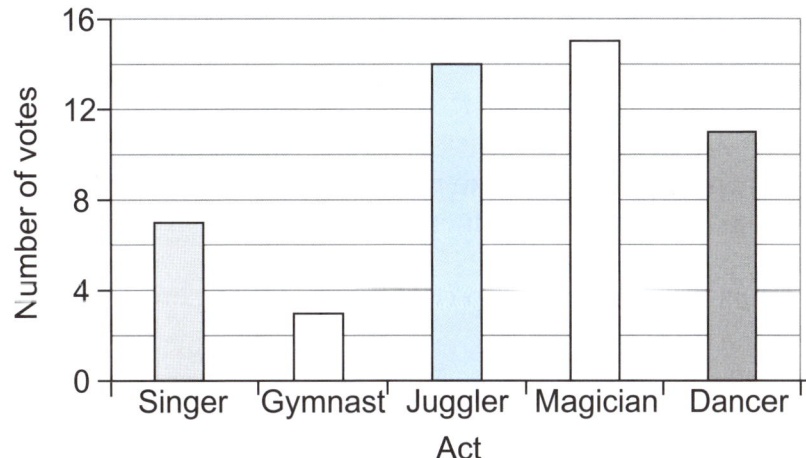

3. Which act got the same number of votes as two other acts combined? Circle the correct answer.

    A   Singer
    B   Gymnast
    C   Juggler
    D   Magician
    E   Dancer

4. What is the ratio of votes for the magician to votes for the gymnast? Give your answer in its simplest form.

5. A spinner numbered 1-10 is shown below.

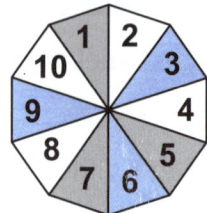

How many numbers on the spinner are factors of both 24 and 30?

6. Raj makes the sequence of patterns below.

Pattern 1    Pattern 2 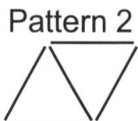   Pattern 3 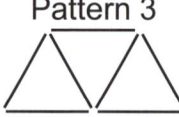   Pattern 4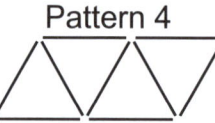

How many lines will there be in Pattern 10?

Andy is taking part in a long-distance bike race. Riders start at 6 am on Monday and must have finished by 4 pm on Wednesday.

7. How many hours does Andy have to complete the race?

 hours

8. Over the first four hours of the race, Andy rode 136 km.
What was the mean distance he cycled each hour during that part of the race?

 km

9. 8 km is approximately 5 miles.
What is 136 km approximately equal to in miles? Circle the correct answer.

    A 68 miles   **C** 110 miles   **E** 211 miles
    B 85 miles   **D** 150 miles

A rat cage is shown below.

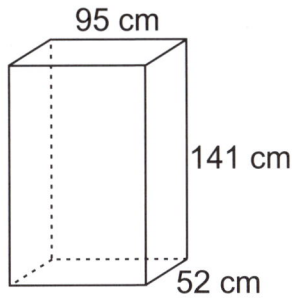

10. What is the area of the floor of the cage?

 cm²

11. Each pet rat needs about 0.07 m³ of cage space. Use estimation to work out how many rats you could keep in this cage. Circle the correct answer.

    A 1   **B** 5   **C** 20   **D** 10   **E** 100

12. The graph below shows how y is related to x.

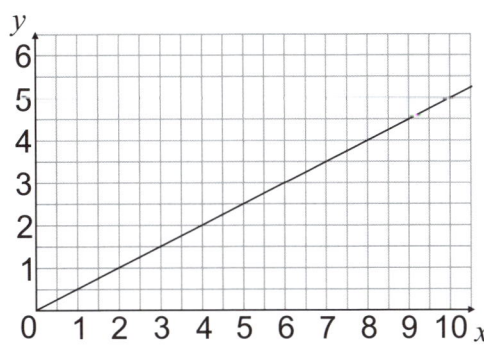

Circle the equation below which shows the same relationship.

    A $y = \frac{1}{2}x$
    B $y = 2x$
    C $y = x + 2$
    D $y = x - 2$
    E $x - \frac{1}{2}y$

Test 13

You have **10 minutes** to do this test. Work as quickly and accurately as you can.

1. What is the least number of extra squares that must be shaded so that the grid has the two diagonal lines of symmetry shown?

   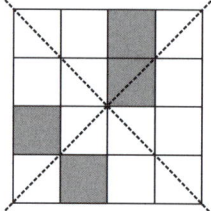

2. Which set of angles could be found inside a parallelogram?
   Circle the correct option.

       A 50°, 60°, 130°, 120°
       B 50°, 50°, 125°, 125°
       C 50°, 50°, 130°, 130°
       D 50°, 50°, 40°, 40°
       E 50°, 60°, 125°, 125°

3. A new pound coin has a thickness of 2.8 mm. An old pound coin has a thickness of 3.15 mm. Sarah builds a tower of 100 new pound coins and a tower of 100 old pound coins. What is the difference in height between the two towers? Circle the correct option.

       A 0.35 mm   **C** 3.5 cm   **E** 35 cm
       B 3.5 mm   **D** 0.35 cm

4. Jon makes a scale model of his pet dog, Floppy. The model is 15% of the size of Floppy. If Floppy is 86 cm long, how long will the model be?

Three identical isosceles triangles are cut from a piece of card, as shown below.

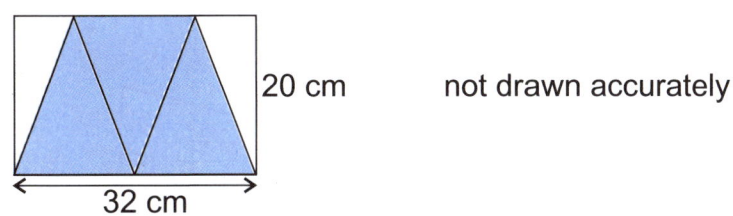

20 cm   not drawn accurately

32 cm

5. What is the area of one of the triangles?

 cm²

6. What percentage of the piece of card is left over after all three triangles have been cut from it?

 %

The petrol tank in Emily's car holds 72 litres when full.

7. Petrol costs £1.11 a litre.
   How much does it cost Emily for a full tank of petrol?

   £

8. The diagram shows how much petrol is left in Emily's petrol tank after a journey.

How many litres of petrol are left in the tank?

☐☐☐ litres

Class 5 are taking part in a readathon lasting seven weeks. The total number of books read since the start of the readathon is recorded at the end of each week, as shown in the graph.

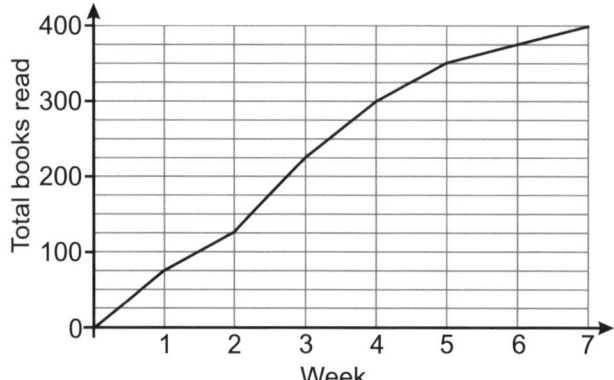

9. How many books were read during the second week? Circle the correct answer.

   A   25   C   75   E   40
   B   50   D   125

10. There are 30 children in Class 5. What was the mean number of books read by each child during the first four weeks of the readathon?

11. If $3(x - 2) = 39$, what is x? Circle the correct option.

    A   34   C   15   E   13.6
    B   13   D   11

12. Steven makes up a sequence. Each term in Steven's sequence is odd. Circle the expression that could give the nth term of Steven's sequence.

    A $2n$ C $2n + 1$ E n^2
    B $3n$ D $2n + 2$

/ 12

Test 14

You have **10 minutes** to do this test. Work as quickly and accurately as you can.

1. £180 is shared out equally between some brothers. Each brother gets £30. How many brothers are there?

2. The net below is folded into a cube.

   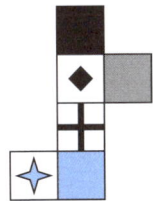

   The cube is placed so that the grey face, , is at the top. Which face is at the bottom? Circle the correct answer.

   A   B   C   D   E

3. Karen counts back in threes from 17. What is the first number less than zero that she will count? Circle the correct option.

   A   −1   C   −3   E   −5
   B   −2   D   −4

4. Ahmed is making fizzy apple juice. He pours 1.75 litres of apple juice into a jug and adds 500 ml of lemonade. He then drinks 150 ml of the mixture. How many litres are left in the jug? Circle the correct answer.

   A   1.9 litres   C   2.1 litres   E   1.6 litres
   B   6.6 litres   D   5.25 litres

The children in a primary school were asked how many of their baby teeth they'd lost. The results are shown in the table.

Number of teeth lost	Number of children
0	30
1 - 3	25
4 - 6	35
7 - 9	20
10 - 12	21
more than 12	19

5. How many children had lost more than six teeth?

6. What fraction of the children hadn't lost any teeth?
   Circle the correct answer.

   A $\frac{1}{4}$ B $\frac{1}{5}$ C $\frac{3}{5}$ D $\frac{3}{4}$ E $\frac{1}{6}$

7. To make a certain shade of green, you mix one part blue paint with five parts yellow paint. Kay wants to have 300 ml of green paint in total. How much blue paint should she use?

   ⬜⬜⬜ ml

8. Pound coins have a mass of 9.5 g each. Sarah puts 100 of them into an empty money box which has a mass of 75 g. What is the total mass of her money box, including coins, now? Give your answer in kilograms.

   ⬜⬜.⬜⬜⬜ kg

9. Hannah runs for 90 seconds, then walks for two minutes. She repeats this six times, starting at 10:49 am. What time does she finish?

   ⬜⬜:⬜⬜ am

10. The volume of this cuboid is 348 m³.

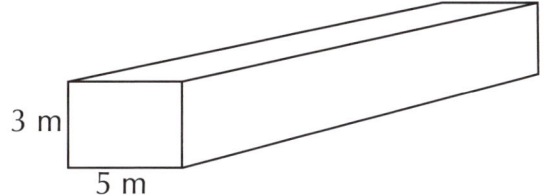

What is the cuboid's length?

 m

11. A triangle on a coordinate grid is translated to a new position as shown.

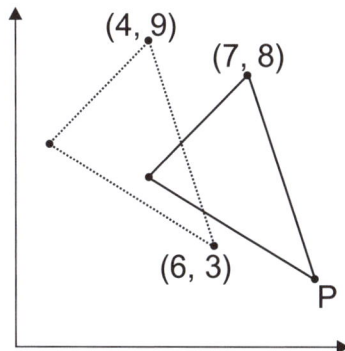

What are the coordinates of point P? Circle the correct answer.

- A (2, 9)
- B (3, 2)
- C (9, 2)
- D (8, 2)
- E (9, 4)

12. A gardener uses the formula $C = 50 + 0.9m$ to work out C, the cost in pounds for cutting a hedge, where m is the length of the hedge in metres.
What will be the cost of having a 20 metre hedge cut?

£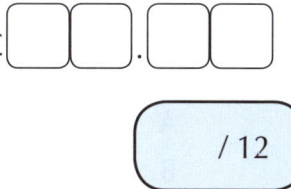

Test 15

You have **10 minutes** to do this test. Work as quickly and accurately as you can.

1. The timetable below shows the times that a bus stops in six different towns. The bus always runs exactly on time.

Broom	Easton	Yew Bridge	Richby	Clayton	Fryton
0852	0927	0957	1014	1039	1104

   How long, in minutes, does it take for the bus to get from Easton to Fryton?

   ☐☐☐ minutes

2. Find the difference between the smallest and largest numbers listed below.

   88.10, 87.43, 87.62, 88.04

   ☐☐.☐☐

3. Look at the diagram below.

   Circle the best estimate for the size of angle x from the options below.

   A 100°   B 200°   C 160°   D 260°   E 181°

4. Clive makes a sequence using the following rule:
   'Subtract 1 from the previous number, then multiply the result by 4'.
   Which of the following could be Clive's sequence? Circle the correct option.

   A 2, 7, 27...   C 3, 12, 48...   E 3, 8, 32...
   B 3, 2, 1...   D 2, 4, 12...

A TV presenter wishes a happy birthday to some children.
The ages of the children who are wished a happy birthday are 5, 6, 8, 2, 4 and 5.

5. What is the mean age of these children? Circle the correct answer.

   A 4.5   B 5   C 5.5   D 6   E 6.5

6. Two of these children are boys. The mean age of the girls is 6.
   How old are the boys?

   ☐ and ☐

7. Jo needs to pack away 1204 Christmas tree baubles. She can fit nine in each box.
   How many boxes will she need?

8. Ranjit makes a pie chart to show the number of cars of each colour in a car park.

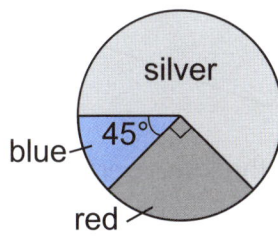

There were 23 blue cars. How many silver cars were there?

9. | 138 × 44 = 6072 |

   Circle the incorrect calculation below.
   - A 138 × 22 = 6072 ÷ 2
   - B 138 × 88 = 6072 × 2
   - C 138 × 11 = 6072 ÷ 4
   - D 138 × 4.4 = 6072 ÷ 100
   - E 138 × 440 = 6072 × 10

10. Ryan is buying some trainers. They usually cost £48 but there is 35% off the price in a sale. Ryan also has a student card that gets him 10% off the sale price. How much will Ryan pay?

11. Darcey is thinking of a number. She says, "The number is a prime number between 30 and 50. It is one more than a multiple of 7."
    What number is she thinking of?

12. The shape below is a kite.

    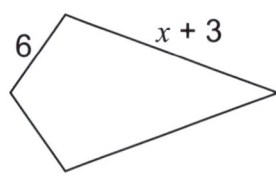

    Circle the expression that gives the kite's perimeter.

    - A $x + 9$
    - B $9x + 9$
    - C $2x + 18$
    - D $9x$
    - E $2x + 12$

Puzzles 3

Now for a break from 10-minute tests. Try out your skills on these puzzles.

Cake Cutting

Six people at a party share a cake. They each have a different sized piece. Use the clues to work out who has which slice of cake.

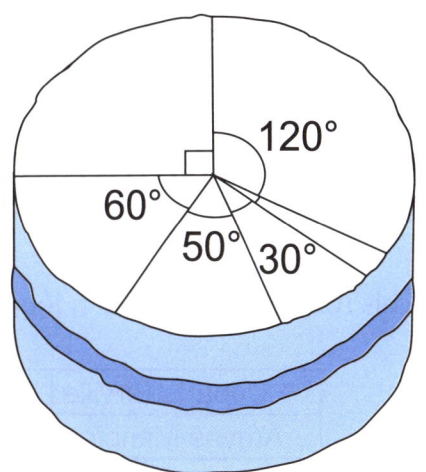

Clare and Dillon together ate $1/3$ of the cake.
Adam and Gosia together ate $1/2$ the cake.
Clare and Fred together ate $1/3$ of the amount that Adam did. Eve ate the rest.

Symbol Sums

In the addition and multiplication below, most of the digits have been replaced by symbols. A symbol that is used in both calculations represents the same digit in both. Each symbol represents a different digit.

```
    △ * ■              ↓ ☆ ♥
  + △ * △          ×       ■
  ───────          ─────────
    * 5 2            ↓ 5 ↑ ⬤
    1 1              7 3
```

Work out which digit each symbol represents and write it in the correct box below.

△ = ☐   ■ = ☐   * = ☐   ☆ = ☐

⬤ = ☐   ↑ = ☐   ♥ = ☐   ↓ = ☐

Test 16

You have **10 minutes** to do this test. Work as quickly and accurately as you can.

1. What number will correctly complete the following calculation?

   _____ × 15 = 30 + 30 + 30

This timetable shows train journey times between the towns of Birville and Mancton.

Departs Birville	0931	0957	1031	1057	1131
Arrives Mancton	1059	1125	1159	1225	1259

2. How long is the train journey between the towns?

    minutes

3. Juliana needs to be in Mancton by noon. It takes her ³⁄₄ of an hour to get to Birville station from her house. What is the latest time she could leave her house to get to Mancton on time?

4. Mel is describing a shape. She says, 'It is an irregular quadrilateral. Its diagonals are always lines of symmetry.'
   Circle the shape is Mel describing from the options below.

   A   Square
   B   Rectangle
   C   Rhombus
   D   Parallelogram
   E   Trapezium

5. Kyle spends the following amounts on snacks each day from Monday to Friday:

   £2.00 £1.00 £1.50 £2.25 £1.25

   What is the mean amount Kyle spends per day?

   £☐.☐☐

6. Which of the following numbers is the same as $^{18}/_8$?
   Circle the correct answer.

   A 1.75   B 2.2   C 2.25   D 2.5   E 2.8

7. In a bag of nuts and raisins, there are four nuts for every raisin.
   There are 96 nuts in a bag. How many nuts and raisins are there in total?
   Circle the correct option.

   A 24   B 100   C 120   D 200   E 216

8. Asif wants to make a cardboard net of the cuboid shown below.

   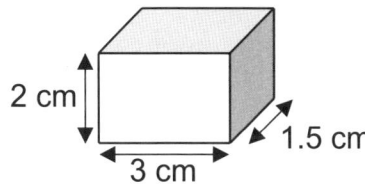

   What will the area of the net be?

   ☐☐ cm²

Jamie sells jam in four different flavours at a market stall.
The chart below shows the proportions of each flavour that he sells in one day.

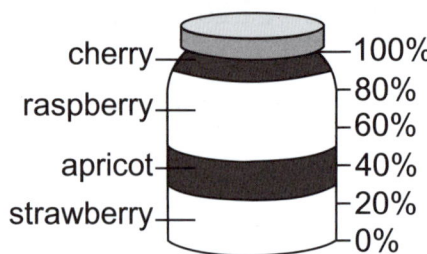

9. Why is the chart misleading? Circle the correct option.
    A   It doesn't show all of the flavours of jam Jamie sold.
    B   It doesn't show how many jars of each jam were sold.
    C   The scale doesn't increase evenly.
    D   The jar narrows at the top, so the top section looks smaller than it should.
    E   The sections are not coloured to match the different jams.

10. Jamie sells 90 jars of jam in total that day. How many of these were raspberry?
    Circle the correct answer.
    A   36   B   40   C   45   D   81   E   90

A phone company charges C pence to make an international phone call
lasting m minutes, where $C = 25 + 6m$.

11. Marco spends half an hour on an international call.
    How much does it cost?

12. Carla spends 85p on an international call that ends at 20:02.
    What time did her call start?

/ 12

Test 16

Test 17

You have **10 minutes** to do this test. Work as quickly and accurately as you can.

1. Eve thinks of a number between 60 and 80 which is a multiple of both 4 and 9. What is the number?

Santino has made 4.5 litres of fruit punch.

2. 1 litre is approximately 1.8 pints. Which of these is the best approximation of the number of pints of punch Santino has made? Circle the correct option.

    A 2   **B** $2\frac{1}{2}$ **C** 5   **D** 8   **E** 20

3. Santino serves the punch in 150 ml cups. How many cups can he fill?

4. The third, fourth and fifth terms of a sequence are: −4, −7 and −10. What was the first term of the sequence?

5. Which of the following is not equal to the others? Circle the correct option.

    A $\frac{3}{4}$ of 36
    B 10% of 270
    C $\frac{1}{2}$ of 54
    D 0.270 × 100
    E $\frac{2}{7}$ of 10

6. Look at the equation below.

   12345 ÷ ☐ = 12.345 × ☐

   Circle the pair of numbers which cannot be written in the boxes in the order given.

   A 1000 and 1   C 100 and 100   E 1 and 1000
   B 100 and 10   D 10 and 100

7. The population of a town is thirty-two thousand five hundred, rounded to the nearest hundred. Circle the largest number the population could be.

   A 32 500   B 32 450   C 32 550   D 32 549   E 31 549

8. The graph below can be used to convert between temperatures measured in Fahrenheit (°F) and temperatures measured in Celsius (°C).

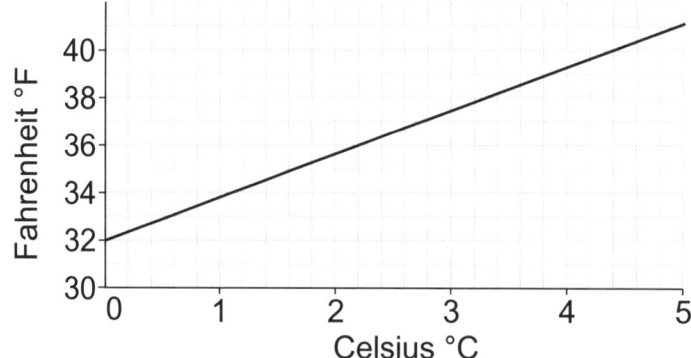

   Use the graph to find the difference in temperature between 36 °F and 40 °F, in degrees Celsius, to one decimal place.

    °C

9. A circle has a diameter of 0.01 m. What is its radius? Circle the correct answer.

   A 1 cm   C 5 cm   E 5 mm
   B 2 cm   D 2 mm

10. A pie shop sells vegetable pies and meat pies. The prices are shown below.

> vegetable £1.50   meat £3.00

One day 50 pies are sold in total.
20 of these are vegetable pies and the rest are meat pies.
The shopkeeper records how much money is made from selling each type of pie.
He wants to show his results on a pie chart. What angle should he use for
the section representing the money made from selling vegetable pies?

°

11. A net of a cube is drawn on a rectangular sheet of paper, as shown.

The whole sheet of paper has an area of 48 cm².
What will be the volume of the cube made from the net?

 cm³

12. Look at the triangle shown on the right.
Circle the equation which is correct
for this triangle.

    A $12y + 20° = 180°$
    B $12y = 360°$
    C $6y = 90°$
    D $12y = 200°$
    E $6y - 10° = 90°$

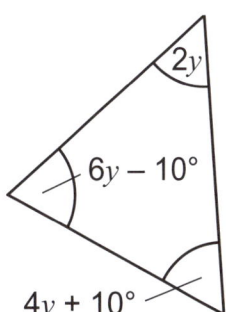

Test 18

You have **10 minutes** to do this test. Work as quickly and accurately as you can.

1. How many rectangular faces does a triangular prism have?

Customers in a pet shop were asked whether they owned a cat or a dog. The partly filled table shows the results.

	cat	no cat	total
dog	26		
no dog			42
total	57		100

2. How many customers didn't own either a cat or a dog?

3. What percentage of customers owned a dog?

 %

4. A point with coordinates (−1, −3) is reflected in the y-axis.
   Which of the points below has the same coordinates as the reflected point?

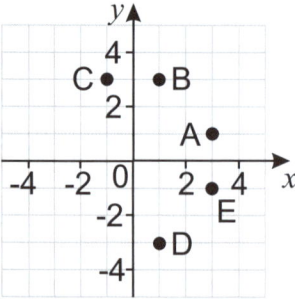

Circle the correct letter.

A   B   C   D   E

5. A piece of string is cut into four pieces. The mean length of the pieces is 10 cm. Circle the option below which does not give possible lengths of three of the pieces.

    A   10 cm, 10 cm and 10 cm
    B   10 cm, 12 cm and 14 cm
    C   1 cm, 2 cm and 3 cm
    D   7 cm, 11 cm and 23 cm
    E   13 cm, 13 cm and 13 cm

6. Work out $4\tfrac{1}{2} - 3\tfrac{4}{5}$.
Give your answer as a decimal.

7. The pictogram on the right shows the number adults (▮) and children (▮) at a sports match.

Both symbols represent the same number of people. There were 1250 more adults than children.

What number does ▮ represent in the key?

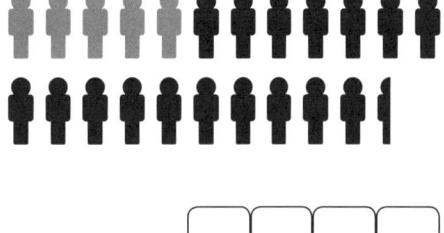

8. The shape below is a parallelogram.

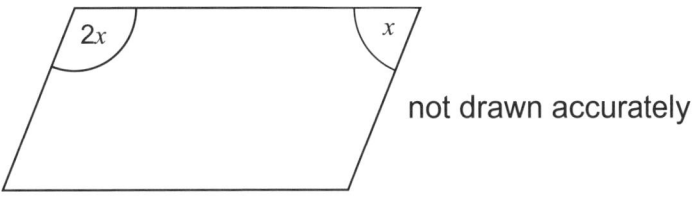

not drawn accurately

What is the size of angle x? Circle the correct answer.

    A   30°   B   45°   C   60°   D   90°   E   120°

Adah is making a large rice dish for 30 people.
She is scaling up a recipe that uses 320 g of rice and serves 4 people.

9. How much rice will she need for 30 people?
   Give your answer in kilograms.

    kg

10. What percentage of the rice will be wasted if only 24 people are served?
    Circle the correct answer.

    A   6%   B   15%   C   20%   D   25%   E   80%

11. A square with a perimeter of 316 mm is cut in half along its diagonal.
    The two halves are rearranged to form a parallelogram, as shown.

    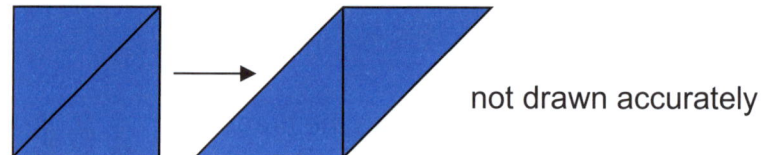

    not drawn accurately

    Find the area of the parallelogram.   mm²

12. A sequence is made of rectangles, as shown below.

    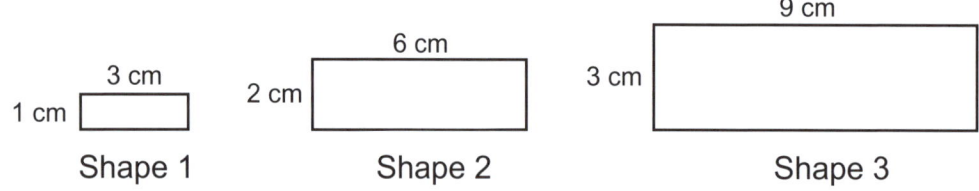

    Shape 1   Shape 2   Shape 3

    Which of these expressions describes the perimeter of the nth shape
    in the sequence? Circle the correct answer.

    A $n \times 3n$ C $n + 3n$ E $8n$
    B $n + n + 3$ D $2(n + 3)$

    / 12

Test 19

You have **10 minutes** to do this test. Work as quickly and accurately as you can.

1. What is 123 456 rounded to the nearest 100?

2. The diagram below shows points Y and Z.

   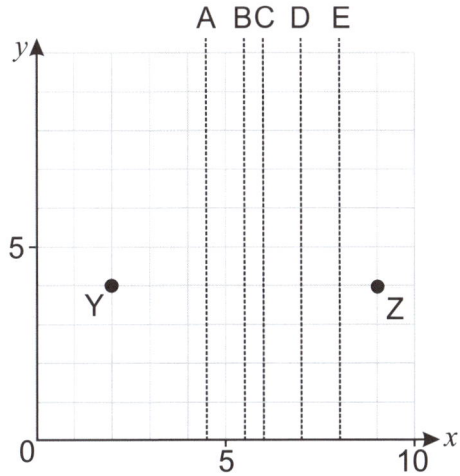

   Point Y was reflected in a mirror line to give point Z.
   Which mirror line, A, B, C, D or E, was this?

3. The seventh term of a sequence is 64.
   Which of the following could not be the start of the sequence?
   Circle the option which cannot show the sequence.

   A 1, 2, 4, 8, 16, ...
   B 34, 39, 44, 49, 54, ...
   C 4, 9, 16, 25, 36, ...
   D 100, 94, 88, 82, 76, ...
   E 8, 17, 26, 35, 44, ...

4. There are two prime numbers between 60 and 70.
   What is the difference between them?

Rose walks along a path through a park.
The graph shows her journey from the start of the path to the end.

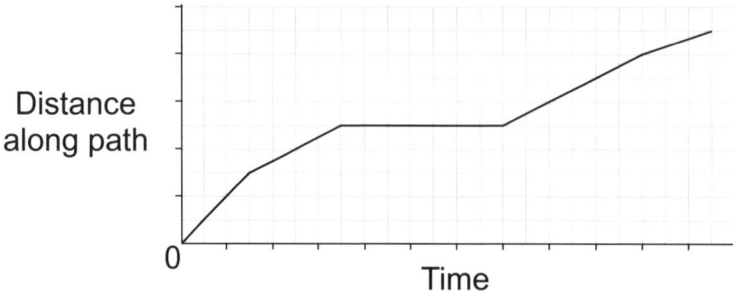

Rose stopped for 3½ minutes at a point 125 m along the path.

5. Which of these statements is true? Circle the correct answer.
   A   Rose stopped after 7 minutes.
   B   Rose walked another 125 m after she stopped.
   C   Rose reached the end of the path after 11 minutes.
   D   Rose walked 225 m in total.
   E   Rose walked for 5 minutes after she stopped.

6. Once at the end of the path, Rose walked back to the start of the path. She took the same amount of time to walk back along the path as she had taken to reach the end of it. She finished the whole walk at 13:07. What time did she start?

   ☐☐:☐☐

Jay has 24 coins in a jar. ⁷/₁₂ of these are 10p coins, ¼ are 20p coins and the rest are 50p coins.

7. What fraction of the coins are 50p coins? Circle the correct answer.
   A ¹/₂₄   B ¹/₁₂   C ⅙   D ⅓   E ½

8. How much money does Jay have in the jar?

   £☐☐.☐☐

Test 19

In a rabbit race, Bugs covers 65 cm with every hop.
The race track is 14.3 m long.

9. How many hops does Bugs take to complete the race?
   Circle the correct option.

   A 2   B 3   C 22   D 200   E 220

10. A carrot is pulled along the race track to encourage Bugs to hop. It is pulled a distance of 0.5 metres every second. How long does it take for the carrot to be pulled along the whole track? Round your answer to the nearest second.

     seconds

11. $41 - 3h = 17$.
    What is h?

12. There are three different paths on a cycle trail, each with a different level of challenge. The pie chart below shows the number of cyclists who took each path, out of a total of 80 cyclists.

    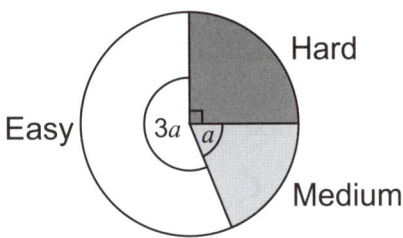

    How many cyclists took the easy path?

Test 20

You have **10 minutes** to do this test. Work as quickly and accurately as you can.

1. Deena had a negative amount of money in her bank account. She then paid in twenty-seven pounds, which made the amount of money in the account positive. Which of the following could be the amounts in Deena's bank account before and after she paid in the money? Circle the correct option.

    A   −£5 and +£32
    B   −£7 and +£21
    C   −£8 and +£19
    D   −£9 and +£19
    E   −£9 and +£17

2. What is the volume of the cuboid shown below?

    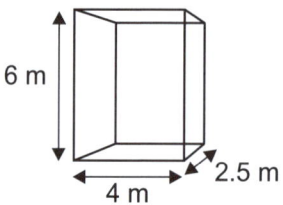

    m^3

3. Five friends share $\frac{1}{3}$ of a loaf of bread equally.
   What fraction of the whole loaf does each person get? Circle the correct answer.

    A $\frac{5}{3}$ B $\frac{3}{5}$ C $\frac{1}{8}$ D $\frac{1}{9}$ E $\frac{1}{15}$

4. The sum of the angles inside a regular octagon is 1080°.
   What is the size of each angle?

    °

Pupils in Year 6 were asked how many pets they owned. The results are shown in the bar chart.

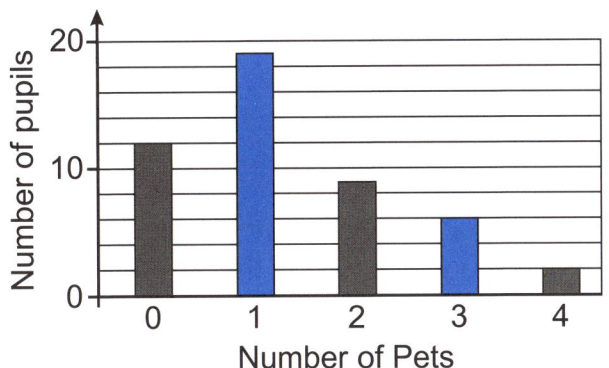

5. What fraction of the pupils owned at least three pets? Circle the correct answer.

   A $\frac{1}{24}$ B $\frac{1}{6}$ C $\frac{1}{8}$ D $\frac{1}{3}$ E $\frac{5}{6}$

6. How many pets are owned in total by the pupils in Year 6?

A giant bar of chocolate is 8 squares wide by 20 squares long, and costs £3.80.

7. The bar is shared out between 9 people so each has the same number of squares. How many squares are left over?

8. The bar is reduced in price by 15%. What is the reduced price?

£ ☐.☐☐

Four people record their heights. These are given below:

1.55 m   125 cm   1.7 m   162 cm

9. What is their mean height, in metres?

☐.☐☐ m

10. There are approximately 2.5 cm in 1 inch, and 12 inches in 1 foot. What is the height of the shortest person in the group, in feet and inches, using this approximation? Circle the correct answer.

   A   3 feet 10 inches
   B   4 feet 2 inches
   C   5 feet
   D   5 feet 2 inches
   E   5 feet 10 inches

The square and rectangle below have the same area.

11. Circle the expression below which does not represent this area.

   A $a \times a$ C a^2 E $2b + 5$
   B $b(b + 5)$ D $b(5 + b)$

12. b is a whole number.
    If $a = 6$ cm, what is b?

☐☐ cm

Test 20

Puzzles 4

Now for a break from 10-minute tests. Try out your skills on these puzzles.

In a Pickle

Padma wants to make lime pickle, using up what she has in her cupboard. For every 8 limes, she needs 125 g sugar, 3 garlic cloves and approximately 8 cm³ of ginger. She has the following amounts of each of these in her cupboard:

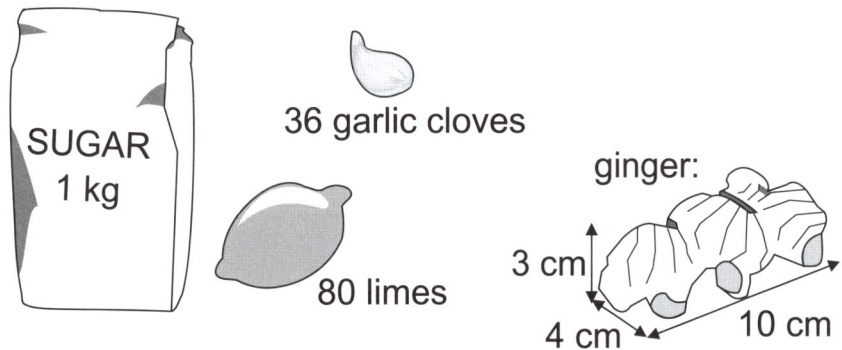

Padma makes as much pickle as possible with what she has in the cupboard. How much of each ingredient above will she have left over?

Riddle Me This

What's my name?

My first is one hundred to a Roman, and my last is a line perpendicular to x on a grid.

My third looks like a shape with a circumference, and my second the symbol for half its diameter.

My fourth is the first of an angle less than 90°, and my fifth is the first of a quadrilateral you can fly.

Test 21

You have **10 minutes** to do this test. Work as quickly and accurately as you can.

1. David makes a sequence of numbers starting with 380. He subtracts 75 each time.

   380   305   230   155...

   What is the next number in the sequence?

Jackson goes to the park for 2 hours.

2. Jackson spends 15% of his time playing on the swings.
   How many minutes does Jackson play on the swings for?

   minutes

3. Jackson leaves the park at 15:48.
   The clock shows the time that he arrives back at his house that afternoon.

   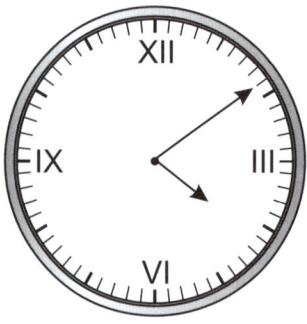

   How many minutes does it take Jackson to get home?

   minutes

4. Leina eats $1/4$ of a cake. Jonathan eats $2/5$ of the same cake.
   What fraction of the cake have they eaten in total? Circle the correct option.

   A $3/9$ **B** $6/9$ **C** $2/20$ **D** $7/20$ **E** $13/20$

5. Kelly chooses two of the cards shown below.

    | 5 | 7 | 9 | 11 |

    She multiplies the numbers on her two cards together and then subtracts 7.
    She rounds the result to the nearest 10. Her answer is 50.
    Which two cards did Kelly choose? Circle the correct option.

    A   5 and 9   C   7 and 9   E   9 and 11
    B   5 and 11   D   7 and 11

Jimmy asked the pupils at his school if they like football, tennis and swimming. He recorded the number of people who like each sport in a Venn diagram.

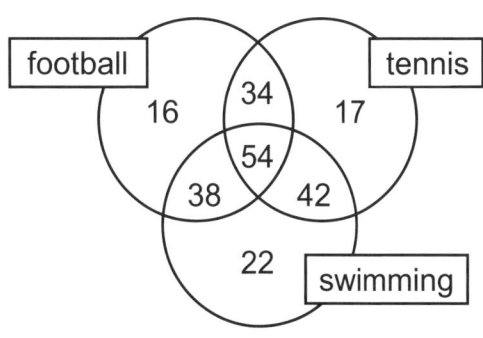

6. How many of the pupils like tennis?

7. How many of the pupils don't like football?

8. Benji is at an ice cream parlour. The menu is shown below.

Menu	
2 scoops of ice cream	£2.40
Additional scoops	£0.90 each
Toppings (sprinkles, sauce, marshmallows)	£0.55 each

    Benji has £7.40 to spend.
    He buys 4 scoops of ice cream with sprinkles and marshmallows.
    How much money does Benji have left?

    £ ☐.☐☐

9. Skyla and Paloma take part in a race.
Skyla runs at a constant speed and covers a distance of 10 km every hour.
Paloma runs at a constant speed and covers a distance of 12 km every hour.
How much further than Skyla has Paloma run after 15 minutes?

 km

10. Callie is facing North (N). She makes the following turns.

   - 135° anti-clockwise.
   - 45° clockwise.

   Circle the direction that Callie is now facing.

   A   NE   C   W   E   S
   B   NW   D   SE

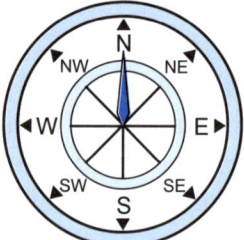

11. Claire has 5 different right-angled triangles.
Which of her triangles is the tallest? Circle the correct option.

   A   A triangle with a base of 6 cm and an area of 21 cm².
   B   A triangle with a base of 5 cm and an area of 20 cm².
   C   A triangle with a base of 3 cm and an area of 15 cm².
   D   A triangle with a base of 8 cm and an area of 8 cm².
   E   A triangle with a base of 4 cm and an area of 12 cm².

12. This diagram shows the angles of each sector in a circle.
What is the value of a?

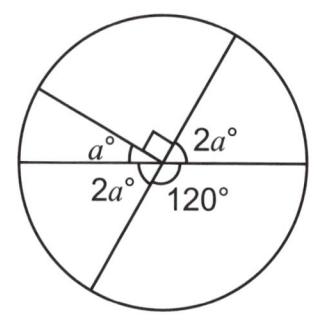

/ 12

Test 22

You have **10 minutes** to do this test. Work as quickly and accurately as you can.

1. Sharon buys five items in a shop. Which of the following shows the prices in order of size, starting from the smallest? Circle the correct option.

   A   45p   £4.50   £4.05   £0.54   £5.40
   B   45p   £0.54   £4.05   £4.50   £5.40
   C   £0.54   45p   £4.05   £4.50   £5.40
   D   45p   £0.54   £4.05   £5.40   £4.50
   E   £0.54   45p   £5.40   £4.05   £4.50

2. Brenda has a piece of ribbon that is 1 m long. She cuts off 4 cm of ribbon. She then cuts the remaining piece of ribbon into 8 equal lengths. How long is each of these 8 equal lengths?

    cm

3. Kian is sorting some numbers into a table.

	Even	Odd
Multiple of 9		
Multiple of 7		

   Circle the group of numbers below that would be sorted into the grey box.

   A   21, 42, 49   C   21, 35, 77   E   18, 45, 81
   B   27, 45, 81   D   14, 42, 54

4. Circle the fraction below that is bigger than $3/5$.

   A $13/20$ C $6/10$ E $8/15$
   B $1/6$ D $3/6$

5. Tamwar is measuring 2 of his toy cars.

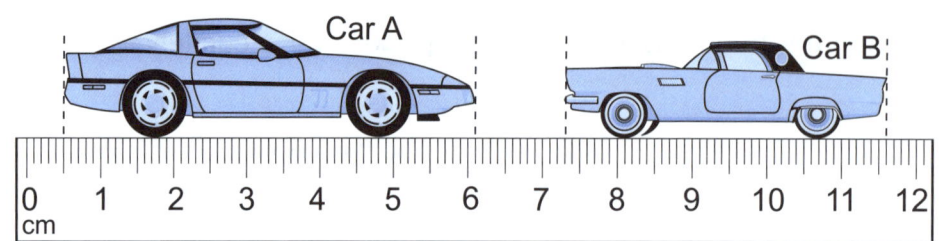

How much bigger is Car A than Car B? Give your answer in mm.

 mm

6. Hazel draws the shape to the right.
She reflects the shape in Line Y.

Which of the following shows her new shape?
Circle the correct option.

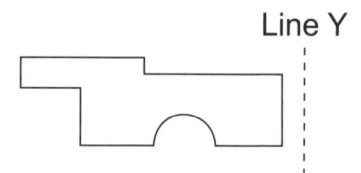

7. Tahlia records the eye colour of 72 pupils in Year 6.
6 pupils have hazel eyes.
Circle the number of pupils that have green eyes.

    A   9
    B   12
    C   15
    D   18
    E   21

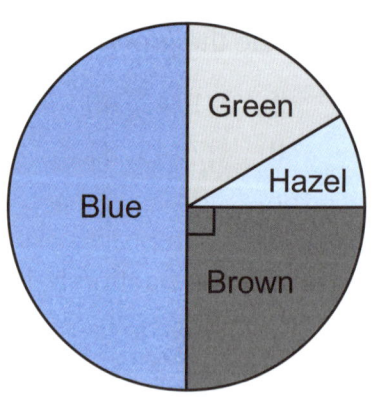

8. Chernice has a jar containing 500 g of jelly beans. 23% of the jelly beans are red. 47% of the jelly beans are blue. The rest of the jelly beans are green.
How much do the green jelly beans weigh?

☐☐☐ g

Juanita buys m packs of stickers. Sanjit buys 4 more packs of stickers than Juanita.

9. Circle the expression which shows how many packs of stickers they bought in total.

    A $m + 4$ B $5m$ C $2m + 4$ D $2(m + 4)$ E $4m + 2$

10. They bought 16 packs of stickers in total.
How many packs of stickers did Sanjit buy?

☐☐

A group of five children are selling homemade lemonade.
The pictogram shows how many cups of lemonade each child has sold.

Jenson	🍋🍋🍋◁
Carlton	🍋🍋🍋🍋🍋🍋◁
Bella	🍋🍋🍋
Casey	🍋🍋🍋🍋◁

Key: 🍋 = 4 cups

11. Each cup sold contains 220 ml of lemonade.
How many more litres has Carlton sold than Casey?

☐.☐☐ litres

12. The ingredients for the lemonade cost £15.90.
The children sell each cup of lemonade for £1.20.
How much profit have the children made in total?

£☐☐.☐☐

/ 12

Test 23

You have **10 minutes** to do this test. Work as quickly and accurately as you can.

1. 100 × ____ = 3640

    What is the missing value? Circle the correct option.

    A 364   B 36.4   C 3.64   D 364000   E 36400

2. The contents page of a book is shown below. It shows what page each chapter in the book starts on. The book is 227 pages long.
    Which is the longest chapter? Circle the correct option.

    A Chapter 1
    B Chapter 2
    C Chapter 3
    D Chapter 4
    E Chapter 5

    Contents
    Chapter 1............1
    Chapter 2..........31
    Chapter 3..........76
    Chapter 4........134
    Chapter 5........185

Some of the angles in the diagram below have been labelled.

3. Which angles are acute?
    Circle the correct option.

    A Angle *d*, Angle *f* and Angle *g*
    B Angle *e*, Angle *f* and Angle *h*
    C Angle *d* and Angle *g*
    D Angle *d* and Angle *f*
    E Angle *f*, Angle *g* and Angle *h*

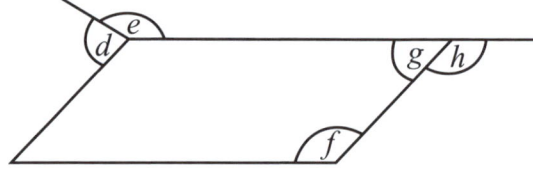

4. Angle *g* is 46°. What is the size of Angle *h*?

5. John and Robyn walk together across the playground.
    For every 2 steps that John takes, Robyn takes 3 steps.
    If John takes 54 steps, how many steps does Robyn take?

6. A pack of 6 beef burgers costs £4.20.
    A pack of 5 lamb burgers costs £3.00.
    How much more does one beef burger cost than one lamb burger?

    £ ☐.☐☐

The timeline below shows what time Giovanna eats her meals each day.

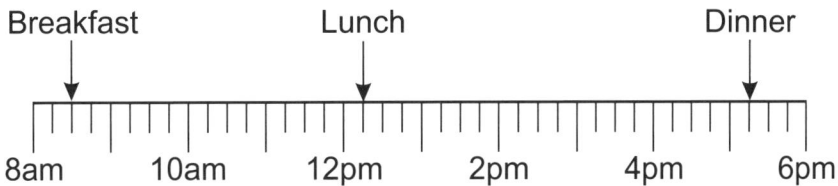

7. Giovanna goes to the park 1 hour and 20 minutes before she has lunch.
    What time does she go to the park?

    ☐☐:☐☐ am

8. Giovanna takes 25 minutes to eat her lunch. She then watches a film for
    1 hour and 30 minutes and then does some painting for 1 hour and 55 minutes.
    When she finishes painting, how long does she have to wait until dinner time?

    ☐ hour(s) ☐☐ mins

9. The diagram below shows the coordinates of each corner of a rectangle.

    Which of the following points
    will be inside the rectangle?
    Circle the correct option.

    A (−65, −32)
    B (−17, 36)
    C (23, −23)
    D (18, 30)
    E (41, 6)

    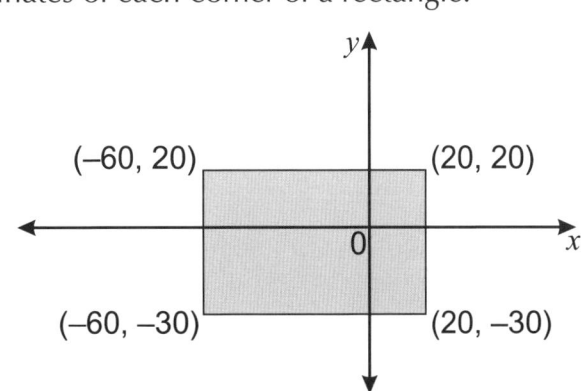

10. Use estimation to work out the number that is halfway between 342.6 and 1393.8. Circle the correct option.

    A   736.2
    B   783.7
    C   868.2
    D   899.2
    E   922.5

The bar chart shows the number of points competitors scored in a sports competition.

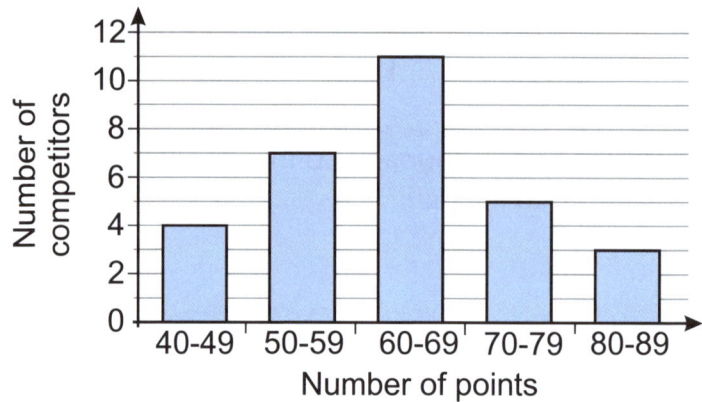

11. The mean number of points scored by each competitor was 63.3. What was the total of all the points scored by the competitors?

12. What might have been the number of points scored by the person who came in 15th place? Circle the correct option.

    A   59
    B   85
    C   76
    D   69
    E   42

/ 12

Test 24

You have **10 minutes** to do this test. Work as quickly and accurately as you can.

1. How many numbers between 10 and 20 are factors of 36?

2. Which of the following pairs of numbers have a difference of 0.37? Circle the correct option.

   A   1.24 and 1.66   C   1.0 and 4.7   E   9.22 and 9.58
   B   0.31 and 0.38   D   4.81 and 5.18

Eliza is making cornflake cakes.
The ingredients for making 18 cornflake cakes are shown below.

Ingredients

To make 18 cakes.

75 g butter
150 g chocolate
4.5 tbsp golden syrup
150 g cornflakes

Eliza only has 50 g of butter.

3. How many grams of chocolate will she need to use?   g

4. How many cakes can Eliza make?

5. Zoe is describing a type of quadrilateral.
It has a pair of equal parallel sides which are a different length to another pair of equal parallel sides.
Half of its angles are acute and the other half are obtuse.

What shape is Zoe describing? Circle the correct option.

   A parallelogram   C square   E trapezium
   B rectangle   D rhombus

6. What is $2^3 + 3^2 + 3^3 + 5^2$?

7. Callum is making a dice from a net. Opposite sides of a dice add up to 7. Which net must he use? Circle the correct option.

2	4	
	5	6
	3	
	1	

A

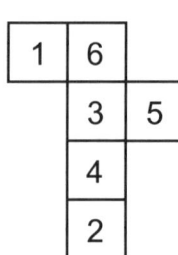

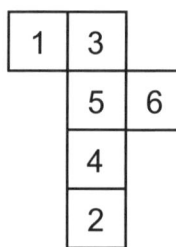

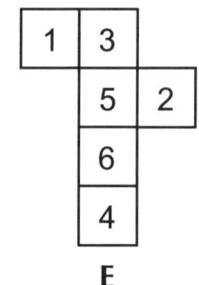

8. The kite on the right is enlarged by a scale factor of 2.5. What is the perimeter of the enlarged kite? Circle the correct answer.

   A 5.2 cm
   B 13 cm
   C 16.25 cm
   D 32.5 cm
   E 39 cm

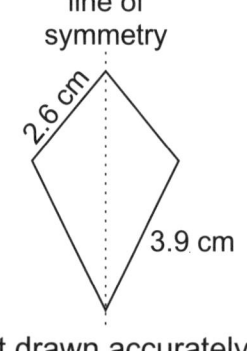

not drawn accurately

A cinema shows 'A Dog's Life' once a day for a week.
The table below shows the number of tickets sold on each weekday.

Ticket	Monday	Tuesday	Wednesday	Thursday	Friday
Adult	19	28	21	13	33
Child	47	54	30	16	37
Family (2 adults and 2 children)	7	26	9	3	11

9. All the adults who had a ticket saw the film.
   How many more adults saw the film on Friday than saw it on Monday?

10. Adult tickets are £10, child tickets are £6 and family tickets are £25.
    How much money did the cinema make from 'A Dog's Life' tickets on Thursday?

    £

11. The pie chart shows sales of the different types of cinema tickets for one day.

    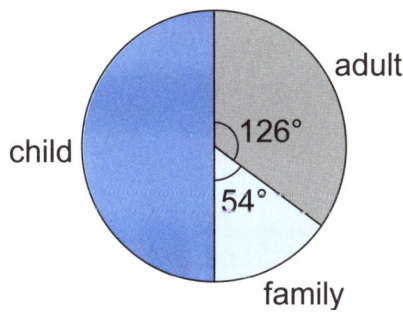

    Which day does the pie chart show? Circle the correct option.

    A   Monday   C   Wednesday   E   Friday
    B   Tuesday   D   Thursday

12. Marley writes an expression.
    When $x = 7$ and $y = 3$, the value of the expression is 84.
    Circle Marley's expression from the options below.

    A $6x + 12y$ C $4xy$ E $5xy - 10$
    B $7x + y^2 + 15$ D $x^2 + 4y - xy$

Test 25

You have **10 minutes** to do this test. Work as quickly and accurately as you can.

Kim has 560 beads for making necklaces.

1. Kim divides the beads into 7 equal piles. How many beads are in each pile?

2. Kim puts 50 beads on some string. Each bead is 13 mm long. What is the total length of beads?

    mm

3. Angelee makes the shape on the right from 9 cubes. She paints spots on the side faces of the shape and leaves the top and bottom faces blank. She then separates the shape back into 9 cubes.

   How many cubes have exactly two spotted faces?

   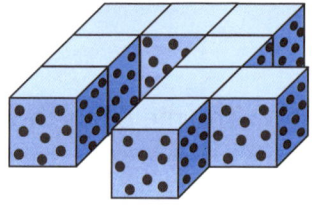

4. A shape has been draw onto the grid below. One of the corners of the shape has been labelled with a cross. The shape is reflected in the y-axis. What are the new coordinates of the labelled corner?

   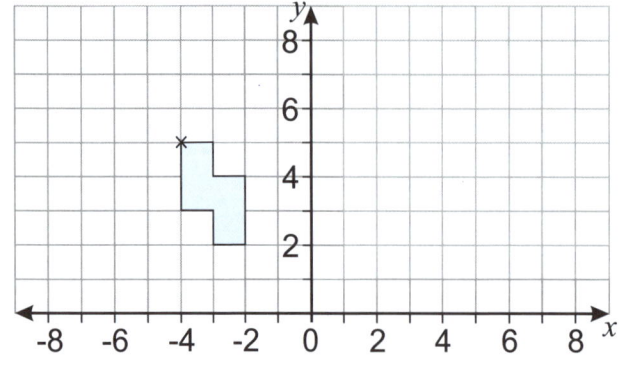

The pupils at Pobbleton Primary School earn stars for good behaviour in a lesson.
The stars earned by 36 girls and 28 boys in a day are shown on the pie charts below.

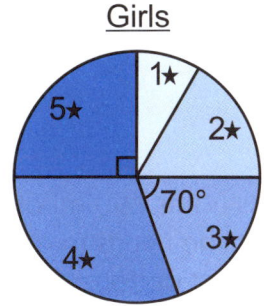
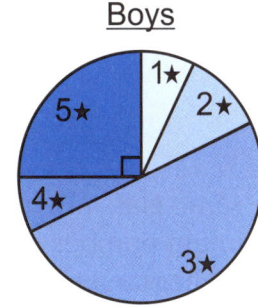

5. Which of the following statements is true? Circle the correct option.

   A   The same number of boys and girls got 5 stars.
   B   Two more girls than boys got 5 stars.
   C   70% of the girls got fewer than 5 stars.
   D   Half of the children got 5 stars.
   E   Eighteen pupils got 5 stars.

6. How many more boys than girls earned exactly 3 stars?

7. A design is made up of regular octagons and squares.
   Each octagon has a perimeter of 24 cm.
   What is the perimeter of the shaded region in the design?
   Circle the correct option.

   A   39 cm   C   48 cm   E   72 cm
   B   45 cm   D   63 cm

   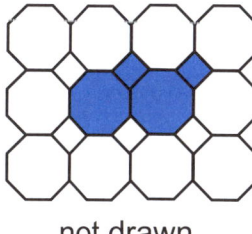

   not drawn accurately

8. Connie is thinking of two prime numbers between 1 and 20.
   The difference between them is 10.
   She adds the two numbers together. Her answer is 24.
   What two numbers is Connie thinking of?

   ☐☐ and ☐☐

Dulcie aims to drink at least 2 litres of water every day.

9. So far today, Dulcie has drunk 460 ml of water.
   What percentage of her target water volume has Dulcie drunk?

10. Dulcie uses the same glass all day. The glass holds 290 ml of water.
    What is the minimum number of glasses that she needs to drink throughout the whole day to meet her target? Circle the correct option.

    A 5   C 8   E 6
    B 7   D 10

11. Martha is weighing some of her toys.

    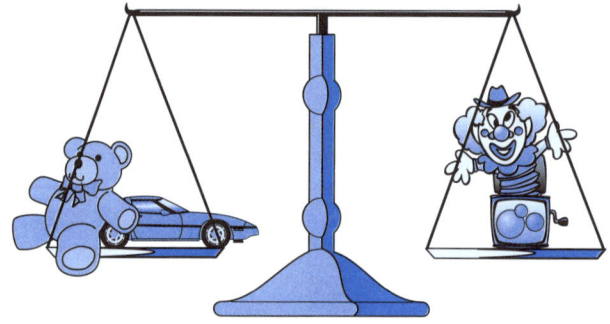

    The teddy and the car weigh the same as the jack-in-the-box.
    The toys weigh 894 g in total. The car weighs 182 g.
    How many kilograms does the teddy weigh?

12. Manoj thinks of a number.
    He puts the number into the formula $2(x^2 - 14)$ in place of x. His answer is 44.
    What number is Manoj thinking of? Circle the correct option.

    A 4   C 9   E 18
    B 6   D 10

/ 12

Puzzles 5

Now for a break from 10-minute tests. Try out your skills on this puzzle.

Percy's Picture Puzzle

Percy needs some help putting a picture of his pet back together.

Each piece of the puzzle contains a maths problem and part of the picture. Help Percy put the picture back together by finding the box in the grid which contains the correct answer and drawing in the correct part of the picture.

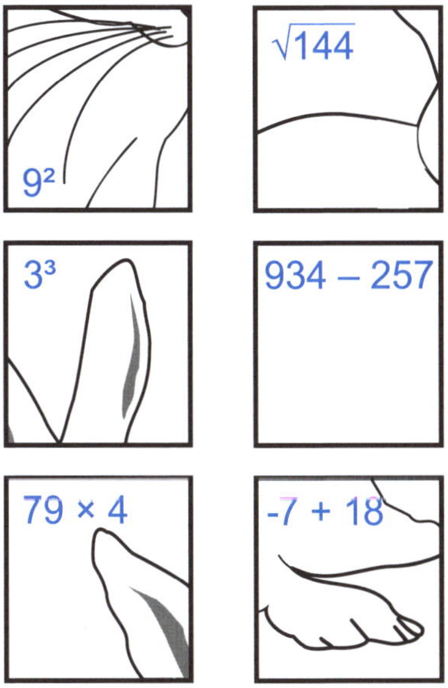

677	316	27	1231
58	12	8	-18
66	540	81	2.5
163	11	7	36

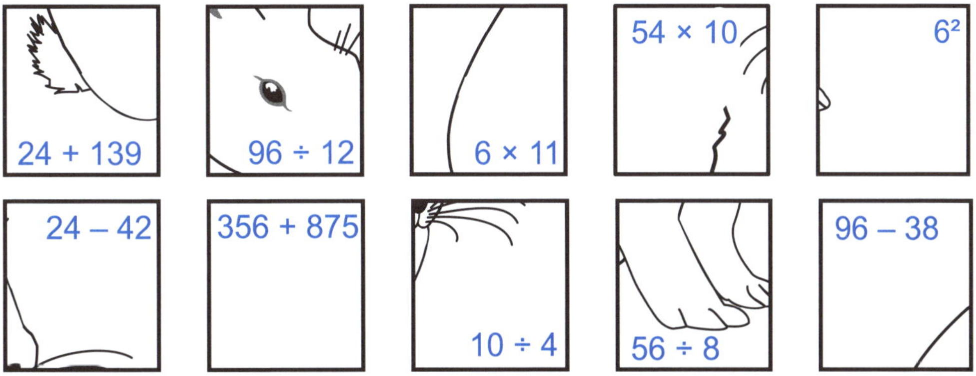

Puzzle pieces:
- 9^2
- $\sqrt{144}$
- 3^3
- $934 - 257$
- 79×4
- $-7 + 18$
- $24 + 139$
- $96 \div 12$
- $24 - 42$
- $356 + 875$
- 6×11
- 54×10
- 6^2
- $10 \div 4$
- $56 \div 8$
- $96 - 38$

Test 26

You have **10 minutes** to do this test. Work as quickly and accurately as you can.

1. Taz receives a cheque for seven hundred and four thousand, three hundred and five pounds and eight pence.
   Write this amount in figures.

2. The first five terms in a sequence are: 2, 5, 8, 11 and 14.
   What is the 10th term?

3. Louis asks the people coming to his party if they are vegetarians, vegans or neither. He makes a pie chart to show the results.

   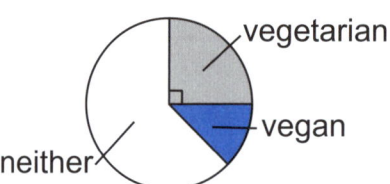

   If there are 6 vegetarians coming to the party, how many guests are coming in total?

4. Owen makes the following table to show how many books of each different type he has on his bookshelf.

Type of Book	Poetry	Fantasy	Sci-Fi	History	Other
Number of Books	3	7	5	2	1

   What fraction of Owen's books are fantasy or sci-fi? Circle the correct answer.

   A $1/18$ B $1/12$ C $1/3$ D $1/2$ E $2/3$

5. A square has an area of 9 cm². What is its perimeter?
   Circle the correct option.

   A   3 cm   C   2.25 cm   E   36 cm
   B   12 cm   D   30 cm

6. An equilateral triangle is shown below.

   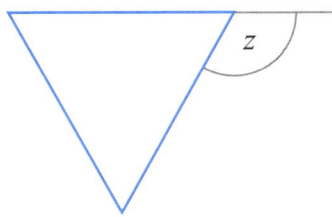

   What is the size of angle z? Circle the correct option.

   A   30°   C   120°   E   Impossible to tell
   B   60°   D   300°

A shape is made on a grid from a rectangle and 4 triangles, as shown.

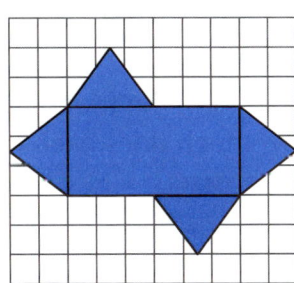

7. How many lines of symmetry does the shape have?

8. Circle the statement below which is false.

   A   The ratio of the total area of the triangles to the area of the rectangle is 2 : 3.
   B   The rectangle takes up 60% of the total area of the shape.
   C   The area of one triangle is $\frac{1}{6}$ of the area of the rectangle.
   D   The area of the rectangle is the same as the total area of 3 triangles.
   E   The area of one triangle is 10% of the total area of the shape.

9. An oven has a width of 76 cm, rounded to the nearest whole centimetre.
It is fitted into a space with a width of 77.5 cm, rounded to one decimal place.
Circle the option which correctly gives the smallest possible oven width and the smallest possible space width.

	Smallest possible oven width	Smallest possible space width
A	75.5 cm	77.55 cm
B	75.49 cm	77.49 cm
C	75.5 cm	77.45 cm
D	76.5 cm	77.55 cm
E	75.49 cm	77.45 cm

A group of seven friends make and sell knitted scarves at a market stall.
Each scarf is made from one and a half balls of wool. Each ball of wool costs £2.60.

10. The group sells 30 scarves for a total of £189.
How much profit do they make in total by selling 30 scarves?

£ ☐☐ . ☐☐

11. At closing time one day, the friends are left with £150 to split equally amongst themselves. How much does each friend get, rounded down to the nearest penny? Circle the correct answer.

   A £20.00   B £20.43   C £21.00   D £21.40   E £21.42

12. $n < 5 + 4 \times 3$

n is a square number.
What is the largest number that n could be?

Test 27

You have **10 minutes** to do this test. Work as quickly and accurately as you can.

1. The diagram below shows the top view of a weather vane, pointing due east (E).

   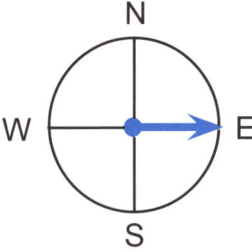

   The wind blows the arrow 270° anticlockwise.
   Which direction (N, E, S or W) is it now pointing to?

2. Mike's cousins have a mean age of 8, and a total age of 40.
   How many cousins does Mike have?

3. Kaitlyn buys a bottle of a fizzy drink, shown on the right.
   The label on the bottle is torn so it does
   not give the units for the volume in the bottle.
   What are the units most likely to be?
   Circle the correct option.

   A   grams   C   millilitres   E   litres
   B   kilograms   D   millimetres

4. In her purse, Dora has twelve 20 pence pieces and eight 10 pence pieces.
   She gives her nephew $\frac{1}{3}$ of the 20 pence pieces and $\frac{1}{4}$ of the 10 pence pieces.
   How much money has Dora given her nephew?

   £ ☐ . ☐☐

5. How many factors of 60 are prime numbers?

6. Lola has $3^3/_4$ packs of chocolate buttons.
   She eats $^1/_5$ of a pack of chocolate buttons.
   How many packs of buttons does she have left?
   Circle the correct option.

       A $2^3/_4$
       B $2^4/_5$
       C $3^2/_4$
       D $3^2/_{20}$
       E $3^{11}/_{20}$

The pictogram below shows the number of different types of tree in a wood.

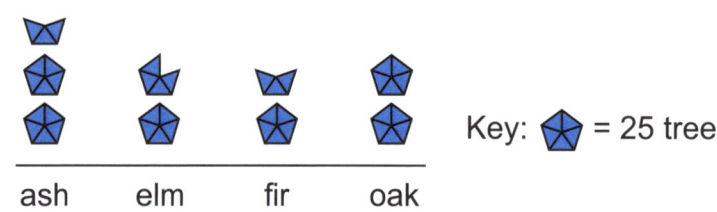

7. How many more ash trees are there than elm trees?

8. What fraction of the trees are fir trees?
   Circle the correct answer.

       A $^3/_5$
       B $^2/_5$
       C $^1/_4$
       D $^1/_5$
       E $^1/_{10}$

9. A regular shape has *x* sides. One side measures 5 cm.
   Circle the expression below which gives the perimeter of the shape.

   A   (*x* + 5) cm   C   (*x* ÷ 5) cm   E   5*x* cm
   B   (*x* − 5) cm   D   (5 ÷ *x*) cm

A number of identical books are to be stacked upright inside boxes, as shown below.

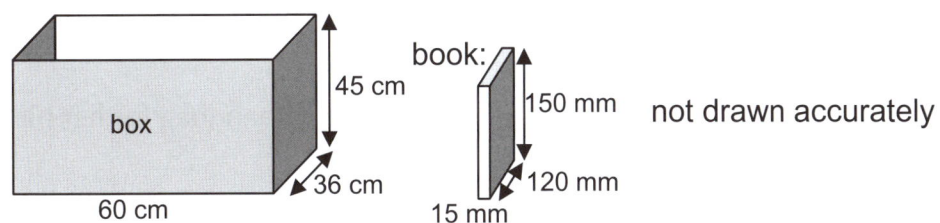

not drawn accurately

10. What is the maximum number of books that can be placed in one box?

11. There are 1200 books in total. How many books will be left over
    if as many boxes as possible are completely filled with boxes?

12. The *n*th term in a sequence is $\frac{1}{2}(n + 1)$.
    Which term in the sequence has the value 5?
    Circle the correct answer.

    A   3rd B   5th C   8th D   9th E   10th

/ 12

Test 28

You have **10 minutes** to do this test. Work as quickly and accurately as you can.

1. An office has 7 boxes of 200 paperclips.
   How many paperclips are there in total?

Noah wants to save up £50 to buy his mum a new handbag for her birthday.

2. So far Noah has saved £16.35. How much more money does he need to save?

3. When Noah goes to buy the bag, it is on sale with 25% off.
   By how much is the bag's price reduced in the sale?

4. Each of the shapes below is a regular shape with a side length of 2 cm.
   What is the mean perimeter of the four shapes?

     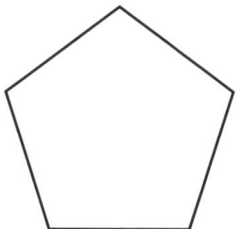 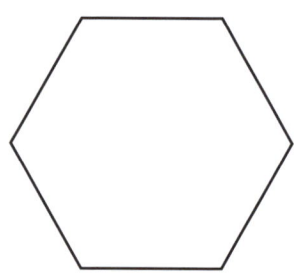

5. The bar chart below, showing the breakfast choices of hotel guests, is missing its frequency scale.

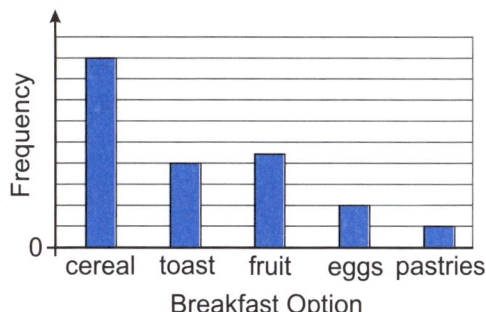

Which of the following could be the frequencies of the five options?
Circle the correct list.

   A   9, 4, 5, 2 and 1   C   18, 12, 9, 6 and 3   E   45, 20, 25, 10 and 5
   B   18, 8, 9, 4 and 1   D   36, 16, 18, 8 and 4

6. The diagram below shows a parallelogram and a rectangle.
   They lie next to each other on a straight line.
   What is the size of angle a?

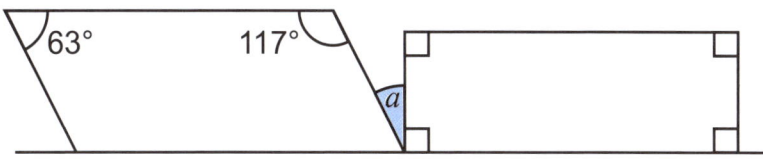

7. At a cafe, Amy pays £4.50 for one coffee and one cake, and Belle pays £6.25 for two coffees and one cake.
   How much will Kate pay for two cakes?

8. Abdul has one third of a full melon. He gives one quarter of his melon to Kendra.
   What fraction of a full melon does Kendra have?
   Circle the correct option.

   A $1/12$ C $1/7$ E $1/5$
   B $1/9$ D $1/6$

9. The table shows the finishing times, in seconds, of five swimmers in a race.

Swimmer	Jay	Kim	Li	Mei	Noa
Time (s)	31.26	29.98	30.04	32.01	30.76

How much faster was the winner than the person in second place?

 s

Four of the lettered points on the grid below form the vertices of a parallelogram.

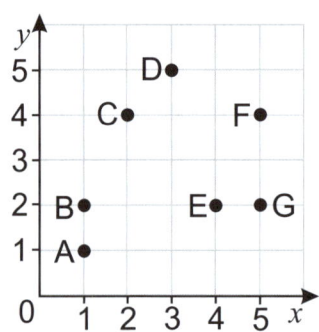

10. Which four letters are the vertices of the parallelogram?
Circle the correct combination.

    A A, B, C and D   **C** C, D, E and F   **E** C, D, F and G
    B B, C, F and G   **D** B, C, E and F

11. Each square on the grid has a width of 0.5 cm.
Find the area of the parallelogram in cm².

 cm²

12. Ollie walks at a rate of w miles per hour.
He wants to walk to the bakery, $3/4\,w$ miles away from his house.
How many minutes will it take Ollie to walk to the bakery and back home again?

mins

/ 12

Test 29

You have **10 minutes** to do this test. Work as quickly and accurately as you can.

1. Kim shares a full packet of biscuits equally between herself, Michael and Sally. The full packet weighed 360 g. How many grams of biscuits does Sally get?

    g

Melanie draws three identical stars. She shades a portion of each star blue.

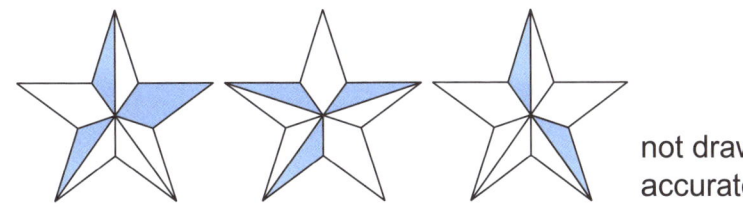

not drawn accurately

2. What percentage of the three stars' combined area has been shaded blue?

    %

3. The sum of the perimeters of the three stars is 240 cm. How long is one side of one star?

    cm

4. | 1 690 834 ÷ 358 = 4723 |

   What is 1 690 834 ÷ 3.58? Circle the correct option.

   A 4 723 000
   B 472 300
   C 47 230
   D 4723
   E 472.3

5. The rectangle below is made from two triangles.
   The area of each triangle is 14 cm². What is the width of the rectangle?

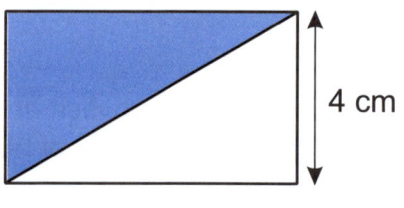

 cm

6. There are 8 bits in a byte, and 1024 bytes in a kilobyte.
   How many bits are in a kilobyte?

A Year 6 class were asked to vote on whether they wanted to play games on the last day of term. The results are shown in the pie chart below.

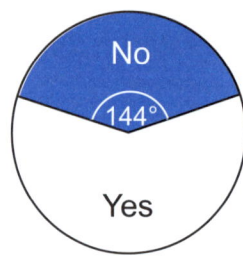

7. What percentage of the class said "No"? Circle the correct answer.

   A   30%   B   35%   C   40%   D   45%   E   72%

8. 12 people said "No". How many more said "Yes"?

9. Alice has £72.00. Elizabeth has £22.50.
   Ella has less than $^2/_3$ of the amount that Alice has.
   She also has more than double the amount that Elizabeth has.
   Circle the amount of money that Ella could have.

   A £35.20   C £46.50   E £55.30
   B £44.90   D £49.70

10. Samantha makes a hexagonal prism from the net shown on the right.
    Circle the corner which joins to corner M.

    A Corner V
    B Corner W
    C Corner X
    D Corner Y
    E Corner Z

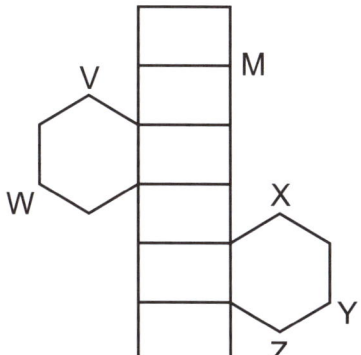

11. 49 000 passes were sold for a festival that takes place over a weekend.
    65% of the passes sold were 1-day passes.
    35% of the passes sold were 2-day passes.
    How many 2-day passes were sold?

12. A mixing bowl has a mass of 90 g. Flour is added to the bowl by the spoonful, with each spoonful having a mass of 10 g. What is the combined mass, in grams, of the bowl and f spoonfuls of flour? Circle the correct expression.

    A $100f$
    B $10f + 90$
    C $10f - 90$
    D $90 + 10 + f$
    E $90f + 10$

Test 30

You have **10 minutes** to do this test. Work as quickly and accurately as you can.

1. What is 10 more than −8?

2. Lenka has some bunches of grapes and a pack of six apples.
Together the apples and grapes weigh 1.8 kg. The pack of apples weighs 700 g.

   What do the grapes weigh?
   Give your answer in kilograms.

3. Lenka eats one apple with a mass of 105 g.
What is the mean mass of the apples that are left?

4. A shop sells a 2 litre container of milk for 97p. Tim buys 14 litres of milk.
How much does this cost him?

5. The diagram below shows a square joined to one side of a regular pentagon.

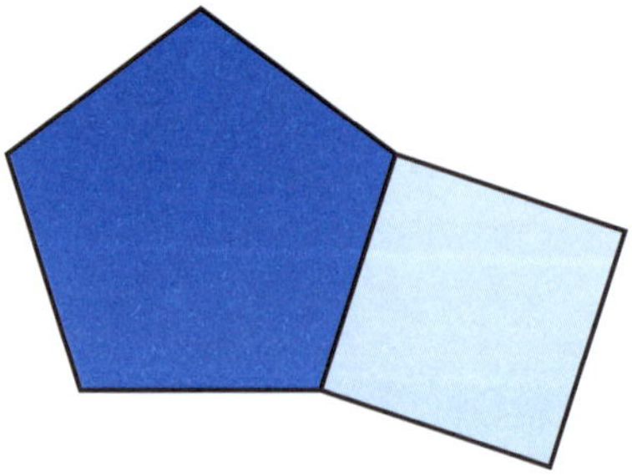

   The pentagon has a perimeter of 35 cm. What is the area of the square?

For one week each year in the school holidays, Nora runs a craft workshop for children. The bar chart below shows the number of children who came to the workshop each day of the week this year and last year.

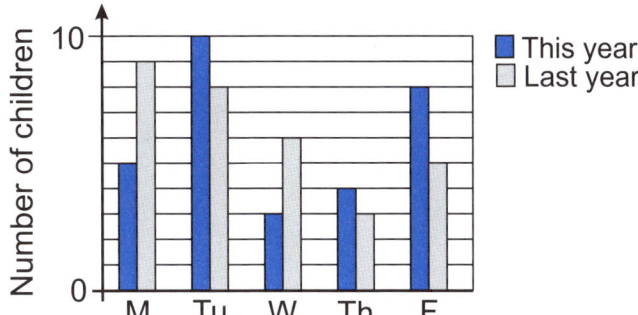

6. How many more children came on the busiest day this year than came on the least busy day last year?

7. Circle the statement below which is not true.

   A Tuesday is the busiest day this year.
   B This year, half as many children came on Monday as on Tuesday.
   C Last year, Monday was three times busier than Thursday.
   D There were 50% fewer children on Wednesday this year than last year.
   E There were more children in total this year than last year.

Farmer Grey only has pigs and cows on his farm.

8. Farmer Grey counts his animals and finds there are 10 more pigs than cows, and 58 animals in total. Circle the number of pigs from the options below.

   A 20   C 30   E 48
   B 24   D 34

9. Farmer Grey counts the animals a few months later.
   The number of pigs has doubled.
   The number of cows has increased by $1/3$.
   How many more pigs are there than cows now?

10. Find the value of a in the diagram below.

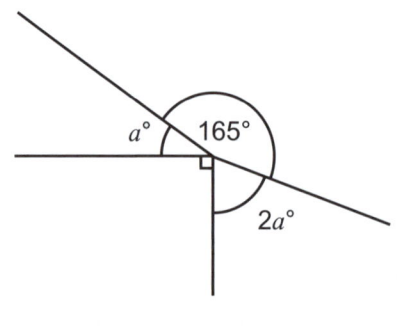

11. Janice wants to buy a new TV. 5 shops have the same TV on sale.
The original price and discount at each shop are shown in the table below.

Circle the shop where Janice can buy a TV for the cheapest price.

A TV World
B Telly City
C Digi-District
D Technoland
E Electromarket

Shop	Price	Discount
TV World	£2000	30% off
Telly City	£1800	25% off
Digi-District	£1600	£150
Technoland	£2100	⅓ off
Electromarket	£1500	£80 off

12. The Translator translates a point with given coordinates by a certain number of units horizontally and vertically, as shown below.

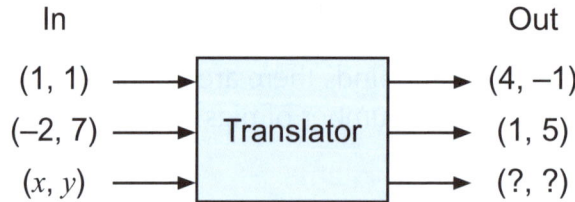

When the point (x, y) goes into the translator, what point comes out?
Circle the correct answer.

A $(4x, -y)$ C $(x + 3, -y)$ E $(x - 3, y + 2)$
B $(4x, y - 2)$ D $(x + 3, y - 2)$

/ 12

Test 31

You have **10 minutes** to do this test. Work as quickly and accurately as you can.

1. 1 kg of strawberries costs £6.50. Leona buys 100 g of strawberries. How much does she pay?

   £ ☐.☐☐

The graph below shows how the temperature inside a freezer changes after it has been switched on.

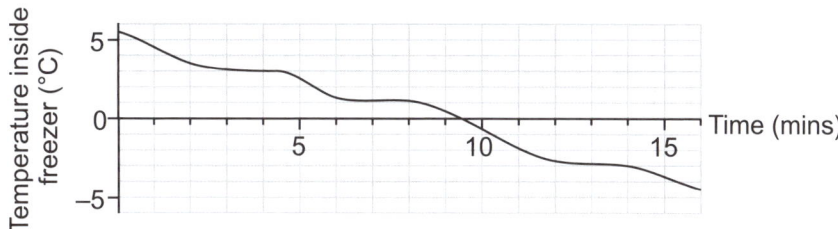

2. After how long does the temperature reach 0 °C? Circle the correct option.

   A   8 mins 30 secs   C   9 mins 30 secs   E   10 mins 30 secs
   B   9 mins   D   10 mins

3. To the nearest °C, how much has the temperature decreased over the 16 minutes shown?

   ☐☐ °C

4. A diagram of a cube and a cuboid are shown below. The cube and cuboid have the same volume. What is the height of the cuboid?

   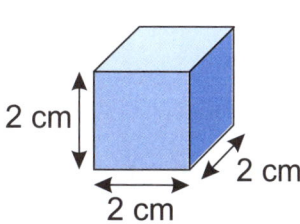
   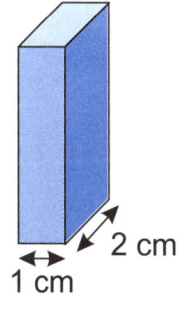

   ☐☐ cm

5. A sequence starts at 32. Each term in the sequence is half of the previous term.
Which term in the sequence is the first to have a value that is not a whole number?
Circle the correct option.

   A 4th   B 5th   C 6th   D 7th   E 8th

6. Jakub arranges 6 candles along the length of a shelf.
Each candle has a diameter of 38 mm.
There is a 15 mm space between neighbouring candles.

   How long is the shelf in mm? ☐☐☐ mm

A florist has 300 bouquets of roses. 20% are pink bouquets, 60% are red bouquets, 15 are white bouquets and the rest are yellow bouquets.

7. How many of the bouquets are yellow? ☐☐

8. Each bouquet has 12 roses.
How many pink and white roses are there in total? ☐☐☐☐

9. What is 685 in Roman numerals? Circle the correct option.

   A CDLXXV   C DCLXXXIIIII   E DCLXXXV
   B DCXIIIV   D LXXXDCV

Test 31

10. Circle the statement below which is incorrect.

    A   0.05 is equivalent to $1/20$
    B $3/5$ is equivalent to 60%
    C   36.6% is equivalent to 3.66
    D   0.7 is equivalent to 70%
    E $1\frac{1}{4}$ is equivalent to 1.25

11. Emma draws the design below.
    The design is made up of a rectangle which contains 4 shaded triangles.
    Each shaded triangle is the same size and shape.

    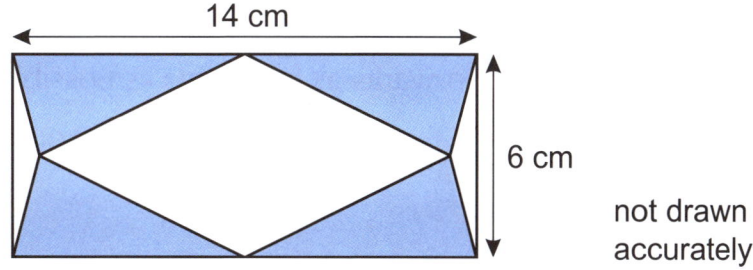

    not drawn accurately

    What is the total area of the four shaded triangles?

     cm²

12. The mean of three numbers is m.
    Which of the following could be the three numbers?
    Circle the correct option.

    A m, $2m$ and $3m$
    B $m - 2$, m and m
    C $\frac{1}{3}m$, $\frac{1}{3}m$ and $\frac{1}{3}m$
    D $m - 5$, $m + 2$ and $m + 3$
    E $m - 1$, $2m$ and $m + 1$

/ 12

Puzzles 6

Now for a break from 10-minute tests. Try out your skills on these puzzles.

Funny Money

In Clown Town, different items are used instead of money to buy things.

The exchange rate for these items is shown on the right.

Daisy is visiting Clown Town. She goes to the bank to exchange her holiday money (£100) for the items she can spend.

 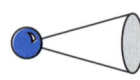

1 nose = £1   1 flower = £2.50   1 horn = £6.50

Daisy only has a small bag, so wants as few items as possible.

What should the bank give Daisy in exchange for her £100?

Painting By Numbers

One corner of the grid below contains numbers. If the number in a box is either square, cube or prime, then shade the box. Otherwise leave it unshaded.

6	14	18	24	32	3	35	28	8	20
15	10	40	45	4	21	2	46	52	7
34	48	12	16	51	30	54	17	38	9
50	13	23	56	22	27	57	58	5	11
29	33	42	55	19	39	25	44	26	1

To complete the pattern, shade boxes throughout the whole grid so that the dotted lines are lines of symmetry for the whole pattern.

CGP

11+ Maths
For the **CEM** test

10-Minute Tests
Answer Book

Ages
10-11

Book 2

M6XPD2E2

Test 1 — pages 2-4

1. C
First compare the digits in the ones columns — the greatest is 4, which four of the distances have. Next compare the digits in the tenths columns of these distances. The greatest is 3, in Adam's and Cho's distances. Compare the digits in the hundredths columns — there's a 5 in Adam's and a 2 in Cho's, so Adam's distance is longest and Cho's is second longest.

2. 4020 mm
Emma jumped 4.02 m. 1 m = 1000 mm, so 4.02 m = 4.02 × 1000 mm = 4020 mm.

3. 2
Obtuse angles are bigger than 90° but less than 180°. There are 2 obtuse angles in one of the new shapes.

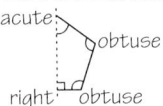

4. £146.53
Add the amounts using the column method.
```
  43.90
  27.63
+ 75.00
-------
 146.53
   1 1
```

5. £1.10
The mean is the total of the prices divided by the number of prices (6). Add the prices in chunks:
97p + £1.03 = £2, £1.20 + £1.25 = £2.45,
£1 + £1.15 = £2.15.
Total = £2 + £2.45 + £2.15 = £6.60.
Mean = £6.60 ÷ 6. Break £6.60 into £6 + 60p.
£6 ÷ 6 = £1, 60p ÷ 6 = 10p.
So £6.60 ÷ 6 = £1 + 10p = £1.10.

6. 480 g
10% of 400 = 400 ÷ 10 = 40 g.
20% = 2 × 10% = 2 × 40 = 80 g.
So the mass of the special offer pack = 400 + 80 = 480 g.

7. C
Both years start MCM, so look at the last part of each:
L = 50, X = 10, V = 5, I = 1
Film A: LXXV = 75, Film B: LXXXIV = 84.
So Film B was made 84 − 75 = 9 years after Film A.

8. B
Farm = 70°, zoo = 90°. Total = 70° + 90° = 160°.
As a fraction of the whole circle, this is $160/360$.
Divide numerator and denominator by 10 and then by 4: $160/360 = 16/36 = 4/9$

9. 18
The 'Bowling' section is 120°. This is $1/3$ of the full circle (360°). 24 children are represented by 120°. So there must be 24 × 3 = 72 children in total (use partitioning). $1/4$ of the children said they wanted to go to the zoo. This is 72 ÷ 4 = 18 children.

10. 6:45 pm
$1^1/_2$ breaks down into 1 + $1/2$. 60 × 1 = 60 and 60 × $1/2$ = 30, so 60 × $1^1/_2$ mins = 60 + 30 = 90 mins.
90 mins = 1 hour + 30 mins.
5:15 + 1 hour = 6:15. 6:15 + 30 mins = 6:45.

11. 6 cm²
Draw point C onto the grid to form a triangle. Find the length of the base and the height of the triangle.

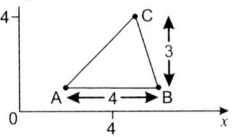

Area = $1/2$ × base × height = $1/2$ × 4 × 3 = 6 cm²

12. D
Angles in a quadrilateral add to 360°.
So 360 = x + 10 + 2x + x + 20 + x = 5x + 30.
Subtract 30 from each side of the equation:
5x + 30 − 30 = 360 − 30. So 5x = 330.

Test 2 — pages 5-7

1. 92
First term = 100, second term = 100 − 4 = 96, third term = 96 − 4 = 92.

2. £4.35
13 breaks down into 10 + 3. 10 × 5 = 50p and 3 × 5 = 15p. So 13p × 5 = 50 + 15 = 65p.
£5 = 500p. 65p = 60p + 5p.
So £5 − 65p = 500p − 60p − 5p = 440p − 5p = 435p.
435p = £4.35.

3. 56 900
You're rounding to the nearest 100 (the hundreds column has an 8 in 56 855), so look at the digit to the right of this. It's a 5, so you round the hundreds digit up to give 56 900.

4. D

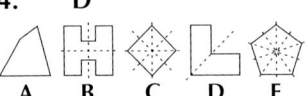

5. D
2040 is 10 times bigger than 204, so 2040 × 7001 is 10 times bigger than 204 × 7001.
So 2040 × 7001 = 14 282 040.
7.001 is 1000 times smaller than 7001, so 2040 × 7.001 is 1000 times smaller than 2040 × 7001. So the decimal point is moved 3 places to the left: 2040 × 7.001 = 14 282.04.

6. B
The sports section for Holly starts at 16% and ends at 88%. 88 − 16 = 72%

7. 45 mins
Reading from the graph, Max spent 30% of the time doing drama. $2^1/_2$ hours = 60 + 60 + 30 = 150 mins.
10% of 150 = 150 ÷ 10 = 15 mins, 30% = 3 × 10%, so 30% of 150 mins = 3 × 15 = 45 mins.

8. 1600 cm²
1.2 m = 120 cm.
So the side length of one slab = 120 ÷ 3 = 40 cm.
Area of one slab = 40 × 40 = 1600 cm².

9. 60
3 slabs make a 1.2 m long path, so find out how many lots of 1.2 m you need to make 24 m.
1.2 × 10 = 12, so 1.2 × 20 = 24 m.
So 20 lots of 3 slabs are needed = 20 × 3 = 60 slabs.

10. 250 cm³
Volume of block = 25 × 8 × 5 = 25 × 40 = 1000 cm³
¹/₄ of 1000 cm³ = 1000 ÷ 4 = 250 cm³.

11. 54°
Angles around a point add up to 360°.
So, $a + 2a + 2a + 90° = 5a + 90° = 360°$,
$5a = 360° - 90° = 270°$.
$a = 270° ÷ 5 = 54°$ (use short division).

12. E
Substitute 4 for x in each expression:
A: $x(x + 2) = 4(4 + 2) = 4 × 6 = 24$
B: $¹/₂(x + 11x) = ¹/₂(4 + (11 × 4)) = ¹/₂(4 + 44)$
   $= ¹/₂(48) = 24$
C: $4x + 8 = (4 × 4) + 8 = 16 + 8 = 24$
D: $8(x - 1) = 8(4 - 1) = 8 × 3 = 24$
E: $5x + 5 = (5 × 4) + 5 = 20 + 5 = 25$
E is the only expression that doesn't give 24 when $x = 4$.

Test 3 — pages 8-10

1. C
A regular quadrilateral has 4 equal sides and 4 equal angles. B, C and D are all quadrilaterals, but only C has equal sides and angles.

2. 5 days
April has 30 days, so April 29th to April 30th is 1 day. Then there are 4 days until May 4th. 1 + 4 = 5 days.

3. D
Half past three in the afternoon = 15:30.
Read off the graph at this time — it is 16 °C.

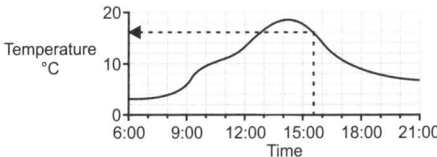

4. 3 : 5
Red pens in a pack : blue pens in a pack = 12 : 20.
Dividing both numbers by 4 gives 3 : 5.

5. 660
Number of red pens = 40 × 12.
4 × 12 = 48, so 40 × 12 = 480.
Number of blue pens = 9 × 20.
9 × 2 = 18, so 9 × 20 = 180.
Total number of pens = 480 + 180 = 660 (add on 180 by adding on 200 and subtracting 20).

6. 105
Mila has 3 circles: 3 × 40 = 120 cards.
¹/₄ of a circle represents 40 ÷ 4 = 10 cards.
Nadim has 2¹/₄ circles: 40 + 40 + 10 = 90 cards.
Mila and Nadim have 120 + 90 = 210 in total. They now have the same number of cards each, so Mila has 210 ÷ 2 = 105 cards (break up 210 into 200 + 10).

7. 100
The total number of circles is $9 + ¹/₂ + ¹/₄ + ¹/₄ = 10$.
So total number of cards = 10 × 40 = 400.
Divide this by the number of children to get the mean: 400 ÷ 4 = 100.

8. 32 km
Substitute 20 for m in formula: $k = (8 × 20) ÷ 5$
= 160 ÷ 5 = 32 (use short division).

9. D
A: ¹/₁₀ of 60 = 60 ÷ 10 = 6, so ³/₁₀ of 60 = 3 × 6 = 18.
B: 10% of 180 = 180 ÷ 10 = 18.
C: ¹/₄ of 24 = 24 ÷ 4 = 6, so ³/₄ of 24 = 3 × 6 = 18.
D: 0.18 × 1000 = 180 — this one is different.
E: 10% of 360 = 360 ÷ 10 = 36,
   so 5% of 360 = 36 ÷ 2 = 18.

10. 10 ml
The number of pancakes she makes is 5860 ÷ 45.
You can use long division to find this:

```
      1 3 0 r 10
45 ) 5 8 6 0
     - 4 5
       1 3 6
     - 1 3 5
           1 0
```

The remainder is 10, so she makes 130 pancakes with 10 ml of batter left over.

11. B
Line CD is parallel to AB, so must be horizontal. Therefore the y-coordinates of C and D must be the same. This rules out options A, D and E.
The difference in the x-coordinates of line AB gives its length. So AB is 8 − 2 = 6 units long. Line CD is half this length, so it must be 6 ÷ 2 = 3 units long.
The difference in the x-coordinates of C and D in option B is 5 − 2 = 3, so option B is correct.

12. B
When reflected in the x-axis, the y-coordinate of A becomes negative, so A has coordinates (2, −6).
Translating it 1 unit left changes the x-coordinate to 2 − 1 = 1. So the new coordinates are (1, −6).

Test 4 — pages 11-13

1. D
The number of tulips must be 3 greater than a multiple of 7. 59 − 3 = 56, which is a multiple of 7 (8 × 7 = 56).

2. −13 °C
Add 5 °C to the temperature inside the freezer:
−18 + 5 = −13 °C.

3. B
The net folds to form a triangular prism.
These two corners meet, so sides B and X join.

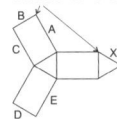

4. 1.25 cm
Each bounce is half the height of the previous bounce.
5th bounce = 5 ÷ 2 = 2.5 cm.
6th bounce = 2.5 ÷ 2 = 1.25 cm.

5. 8
The number of children who chose a chocolate biscuit with juice is 9 − 5 = 4. 12 children chose juice in total, so the number who chose juice and a plain biscuit is 12 − 4 = 8.

6. 30%
12 out of 40 children chose juice: ¹²/₄₀ = ³/₁₀ = ³⁰/₁₀₀ (divide both numbers by 4, then multiply by 10).
This is the same as 30%.

7.   68 cm²
Split the shape into a rectangle and a triangle.
Area of rectangle = 10 × 6 = 60 cm².
Base of triangle = 18 − 10 = 8 cm. Height of triangle = 6 − 4 = 2 cm. Area of triangle = $^1/_2$ × 8 × 2 = 8 cm².
Total area of the shape = 60 + 8 = 68 cm².

8.   14 170 g
Each jar of jam weighs 450 + 95 = 545 g.
The total mass of all the jars is 26 × 545 g:

```
      545
 ×     26
     3270
    10900
    14170
```

9.   D
Find equivalent fractions of $^2/_5$ and $^2/_3$ that have the same denominator:
$^2/_5$ = $^6/_{15}$ (multiply both numbers by 3).
$^2/_3$ = $^{10}/_{15}$ (multiply both numbers by 5).
$^2/_5$ + $^2/_3$ = $^6/_{15}$ + $^{10}/_{15}$ = $^{16}/_{15}$ = $1^1/_{15}$

10.   151°
Angles in a triangle add up to 180°. So the third angle in triangle = 180 − 90 − 61 = 29°. Angles on a straight line add up to 180°. So b = 180 − 29 = 151°.

11.   C
The entry fee is £6, so the expression will be "6 + something". There is a charge per plate of £3.25. For p plates this will be 3.25 × p, or 3.25p.
So total cost = 6 + 3.25p

12.   £3.50
To find the cost of painting 10 plates at Plates R Us, read off the cost of painting 5 plates from the graph.
This is £17.50. 5 × 2 = 10, so painting 10 plates costs £17.50 × 2 = £35.
At Smashers, the cost is 6 + (3.25 × 10) = 6 + 32.5 = £38.50. Work out how much Gina saves by finding the difference between the two prices:
£38.50 − £35 = £3.50.

Test 5 — pages 14-16

1.   120 mm
Regular pentagons have 5 sides of equal length.
So the length of each side = 600 ÷ 5 = 120 mm (use short division or partitioning).

2.   D
Round each number in the calculation to a sensible value: 150 000 − 20 000 = 130 000.
The closest option to this is 128 906.8 — option D.

3.   6.4 cm
The radius of a circle is half of the diameter, so the radius is 12.8 ÷ 2 = 6.4 cm.

4.   A
Add the widths of all 5 items: 1.00 + 2.95 + 2.45 + 1.10 + 0.50 = 1.00 + 5.40 + 1.60 = 8.00 m.
This is 1 m too much, so the 1.00 m bookcase isn't used.

5.   A
$^1/_3$ ÷ 3 = $^1/_9$. So each of the 3 slices on Ruby's plate is $^1/_9$ of the whole pizza.

6.   25.92 m²
Area = 6 × 4.32. 4.32 breaks into 4 + 0.3 + 0.02.
6 × 4 = 24, 6 × 0.3 = 1.8, 6 × 0.02 = 0.12.
So 6 × 4.32 = 24 + 1.8 + 0.12 = 25.92 m².

7.   C
The years go 2002, 2003, 2004, then jump to 2015, 2016. It looks like there's been a sudden drop in bikes sold, when it may have been a very gradual decrease.

8.   6:57 pm
Find the number of minutes between 6:30 pm and 8:45 pm.
6:30 to 8:30 is 2 hours = 2 × 60 mins = 120 mins.
8:30 to 8:45 = 15 mins. Total = 120 + 15 = 135 mins.
$^1/_5$ of 135 mins = 135 ÷ 5 = 27 mins (use short division). $^1/_5$ of the candle had burned 27 mins after 6:30 pm, which is 6:57 pm.

9.   1
To get the mean, the total mark is divided by the number of tests. So multiplying the mean mark by the number of tests gives the total mark. For the first five tests: total mark = 7 × 5 = 35. For all six tests: total mark = 6 × 6 = 36. So marks in sixth test = 36 − 35 = 1.

10.   C
Count back in 8s, from 17: 17, 9, 1, −7, −15, −23
−23 is an option, so must be the answer.

11.   (−3, 1)
Moving one square left decreases the x-coordinate by 1. Moving two squares up increases the y-coordinate by 2. So, new coordinates are (−2 − 1, −1 + 2) = (−3, 1).

12.   B
The number of blocks in the bottom layer of a pattern is the pattern number squared. So the bottom layer of the nth pattern has n^2 blocks. There's always 1 block in the top layer, so there are $n^2 + 1$ blocks in the nth pattern.

Puzzles 1 — page 17
Pyramid Problem
Reading across each row, from left to right, starting at the top: 22, 140, 6, 15, 210, 12, 57, 105, 84, 8.

Test 6 — pages 18-20
1.   B
The 7 in 172.8 is worth 7 tens or 70. In options A, C and E, the 7 is worth 7 ones (7), and in option D, the 7 is worth 7 tenths (0.7). These are smaller than 70.

2.   6
Each small square is worth 8 ÷ 4 = 2 points.
Team D scored three more small squares than Team B.
This is equal to 3 × 2 = 6 points.

3.   B
30 = 24 + 6 = (3 × 8) + (3 × 2) = 3 big squares and 3 small squares, which matches option B.

4.   90 cm
The longer side of the rectangle is 2 × 15 = 30 cm.
So the perimeter is 15 + 30 + 15 + 30 = 90 cm.

5. C
10% of 120 = 12, so 5% of 120 = 6, not 24.
All of the other options make 24.

6. E
150 ml ÷ 1000 = 0.15 litres. 2.5 – 0.15 = 2.35 litres.

7. 12 cm
The area of a triangle is $\frac{1}{2}$ × base × height.
So for this triangle, 24 = $\frac{1}{2}$ × 4 × height = 2 × height.
So the height must be 12 cm.

8. 1105
V (5), C (100) and M (1000) all have one line of symmetry. 5 + 100 + 1000 = 1105.

9. 68
The two primes between 30 and 40 are 31 and 37.
31 + 37 = 68.

10. £9.00
At the weekend, Adam earns £7.00 × 2 = £14.00 per day. In one week he earns:
(5 × £7.00) + (2 × £14.00) = £35.00 + £28.00
                                     = £63.00
So the mean amount = £63.00 ÷ 7 = £9.00 per day.

11. E
The angles a and b lie on a straight line, and angles on a straight line add up to 180°. So $b = 180° - a$.

12. £4.90
If $n = 10$, then $B = (24 \div 10) + 2.5 = 2.4 + 2.5 = 4.9$.
In pounds, this is £4.90.

Test 7 — pages 21-23

1. 17 minutes
The bus will arrive at High Street at 3:04 pm.
2:47 pm to 3:00 pm is 13 minutes.
3:00 pm to 3:04 pm is 4 minutes.
So Dan will have to wait 13 + 4 = 17 minutes.

2. C
19 590 rounds up to 20 000 to the nearest 1000.
A is incorrect because 2499 rounds down to 2000 to the nearest 1000.
B is incorrect because 19 590 rounds up to 19 600 to the nearest 100.
D is incorrect because 20 005 rounds up to 20 010 to the nearest 10.
E is incorrect because 20 500 rounds up to 21 000 to the nearest 1000.

3. 4 cm²
The bottom face of the shape will look like this:
Each square has an area of 1 cm × 1 cm = 1 cm².
So the total area = 4 × 1 = 4 cm².

4. 24
Volume of one of Jill's cubes = 2 × 2 × 2 = 8 cm³.
So volume of 3 of Jill's cubes = 3 × 8 = 24 cm³.
Volume of one of Jack's cubes = 1 × 1 × 1 = 1 cm³.
So Jack would need to use 24 cubes to make the same shape.

5. 2
Use short division to work out 2576 ÷ 9:
  2 8 6 r 2
9) 2 5 ⁷5 ₅6   so the remainder is 2.

6. B
There are 6 divisions between 0 and 2,
so there are 3 divisions between 0 and 1.
So each division is worth $1 \div 3 = \frac{1}{3}$.
The arrow is pointing to 4 divisions past 2.
3 divisions past 2 is 3, so 4 divisions past 2 is $3\frac{1}{3}$ = $\frac{9}{3} + \frac{1}{3} = \frac{10}{3}$.

7. C
The shape can be split into a square of area 3 m × 3 m, and a rectangle of area 2 m × 6 m.
So the total area = 3 × 3 + 2 × 6 = 9 + 12 = 21 m².
The area of the parallelogram in option C = base × height
= 7 × 3 = 21 m².
So the parallelogram has the same area as the shape.

8. 4750
To find Kemi's number, apply the inverse of the steps in reverse order, i.e. subtract $\frac{1}{4}$ from 5 then multiply by 1000. $\frac{1}{4}$ is the same as 0.25, and 5 – 0.25 = 4.75.
4.75 × 1000 = 4750, so the number must be 4750.

9. 43
$6^2 = 36$ and $7^2 = 49$. The primes that lie between these numbers are 37, 41, 43 and 47. The only one of these whose digits have a difference of 1 is 43. So Mark must be 43.

10. 40 km
From the graph, 2.5 miles = 4 km.

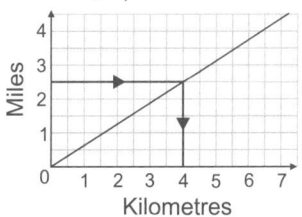

So, scaling up:
10 × 2.5 miles = 10 × 4 km
25 miles = 40 km

11. D
The kite has a vertical line of symmetry, which makes the angle opposite the 120° angle also 120°. Angles in any quadrilateral add up to 360°, so the top and bottom angle will add up to 360° – (2 × 120°) = 120°.
So $x + y = 120°$.

12. E
The sequence starts with $n = 1$, and for the 10th term $n = 10$. E is correct because when $n = 1$, $n^2 + 1 = 2$ (even), and when $n = 10$, $n^2 + 1 = 101$ (odd).
A is incorrect because when $n = 10$, $2n = 20$ (even).
B is incorrect because when $n = 10$, $20 - 2n = 0$ (even).
C is incorrect because when $n = 1$, $n^2 = 1$ (odd).
D is incorrect because when $n = 1$, $2n + 1 = 3$ (odd).

Test 8 — pages 24-26

1. 20p
5 small packets will cost 5 × 80p = 400p.
£3.80 = 380p. So the multipack is 400 – 380 = 20p cheaper.

2.   84 mm
A regular hexagon has 6 equal sides, so if the perimeter of one hexagon is 36 mm, each side must be 36 ÷ 6 = 6 mm. There are 14 of these sides on the given shape, so the perimeter = 14 × 6 mm.
Break 14 into 10 + 4. 10 × 6 = 60. 4 × 6 = 24.
So 14 × 6 = 60 + 24 = 84 mm.

3.   C
The total of the shoe sizes = 7 + 3 + 5 + 2 + 4 = 21.
21 = 3 × 7, so it is not a prime number. So C is not true.

4.   9
If the mean of six sizes is 5, then the total of all six must be 6 × 5 = 30. The total of the 5 known sizes is 21, so the sixth size must be 30 − 21 = 9.

5.   C
C fits the sequence because doubling 3 and adding nine gives 6 + 9 = 15, and doubling 15 and adding nine gives 30 + 9 = 39.
A is incorrect because doubling 1 and adding nine should give 11, not 2, as the second term.
B is incorrect because doubling 11 and adding nine should give 31, not 22, as the third term.
D is incorrect because doubling 2 and adding nine should give 13, not 11, as the second term.
E is incorrect because doubling 1 and adding nine should give 11, not 10, as the second term.

6.   C
After translating the cross 5 squares up and 2 squares left, it now lies on Line S.

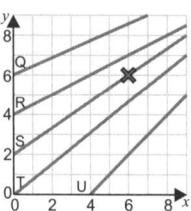

7.   90 s

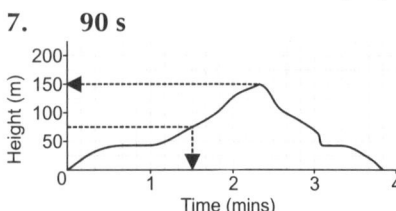

The graph shows that the hill is 150 m high, so halfway up the hill must be 150 ÷ 2 = 75 m. Reading across and down from 75 m gives a time halfway between 1 and 2 mins = 1½ mins. There are 60 seconds in a minute, so 1½ mins = 60 + 30 = 90 s.

8.   15 seconds

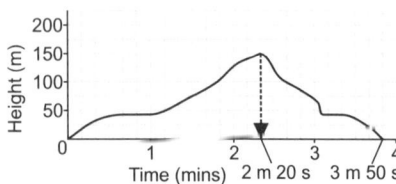

There are six divisions per minute on the time scale, so each division is worth 60 s ÷ 6 = 10 s. It took Kate 3 mins 50 s − 2 mins 20 s = 1 min 30 s to run down the hill. So she ran down the hill 1 min 45 s − 1 min 30 s = 15 s faster than last time.

9.   25 mm
Find the diameter of the smaller bracelet: ⅓ of 75 mm is 75 ÷ 3 = 25 mm, so ⅔ of 75 mm is 25 × 2 = 50 mm. The radius of a circle is half of its diameter, so the radius of the smaller bracelet is 50 ÷ 2 = 25 mm.

10.   C
The ratio of the circumference is ⅔ : 3/3.
Multiply both sides of the fraction by 3 to give 2:3.
So the number of jewels are also in the ratio 2:3.
There are 5 'parts' in the ratio, so the larger bracelet has ⅗ of the jewels. ⅗ of 25 = (25 ÷ 5) × 3 = 15.

11.   D
If $A = 3$ and $B = 1$, then $(2 \times 3) − (3 \times 1) = 3$, meaning the given equation is satisfied.
A is incorrect because $(2 \times 4) − (3 \times 1) = 5$.
B is incorrect because $(2 \times 3) − (3 \times 2) = 0$.
C is incorrect because $(2 \times 3) − (3 \times 3) = −3$.
E is incorrect because $(2 \times 4) − (3 \times 2) = 2$.

12.   15
$B = 9$, so $2A − (3 \times 9) = 3$.
$2A − 27 = 3$, so $2A$ must be 30,
and so A must be 30 ÷ 2 = 15.

Test 9 — pages 27-29
1.   60°
The angles on a straight line add up to 180°.
180° − 120° = 60°.

2.   D
−5.5 °C to 0 °C is 5.5 °C. 0 °C to 4.5 °C is 4.5 °C.
So the total temperature rise is 5.5 °C + 4.5 °C = 10 °C.
A and C are incorrect because they each involve a temperature increase of 12 °C not 10 °C.
B and E are incorrect because they involve a decrease of 10 °C, not an increase.

3.   21
The total who wanted coffee = 65 − 29 = 36.
The number of those who wanted their coffee with milk = 36 − 15 = 21.

4.   D
The fraction who wanted tea with milk = 13/65 = 1/5.
1/5 as a percentage is 20%.

5.   D
There are 5 divisions between 10 and 20 on the frequency scale, so each division is worth (20 − 10) ÷ 5 = 10 ÷ 5 = 2 people. So half a division is worth 1 person. Reading off the bar chart using this scale, the frequencies for each colour are as follows:
Red = 12, Brown = 25, Blond = 16, Black = 24 and Other = 13. 24 is 2 × 12, so black is twice as common as red.

6.   E
The scale starts at 10 rather than 0, so the height of each bar looks smaller than it really is, which makes the differences between the bars look bigger. For example, the height of the 'Black' bar looks much more than twice the height of the 'Red' bar.

7.   25 g
The mean is the total mass of sugar divided by the number of cakes, which is 450 g ÷ 18.
45 ÷ 9 = 5, so 450 ÷ 9 = 50 g.
18 = 9 × 2, so 450 g ÷ 18 = 50 g ÷ 2 = 25 g.

8. 0.675 kg
Total mass = 450 g × 2.5 = 450 g × 2½.
450 × 2 = 900, and 450 × ½ = 225,
so total mass = 900 + 225 = 1125 g.
Mass of the other ingredients = 1125 − 450 = 675 g.
675 g ÷ 1000 = 0.675 kg.

9. 135
If $^2/_3 x = 90$, then $^1/_3 x = 90 ÷ 2 = 45$,
and $^3/_3 x = x = 45 × 3 = 135$.

10. 40 000 mm²
Split the shape up into a triangle and a rectangle:

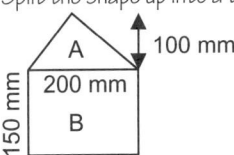

Area of a triangle = ½ × base × height,
so Area A = ½ × 200 × 100 = 10 000 mm².
Area of a rectangle = length × width,
so Area B = 150 × 200 = 150 × 2 × 100
= 300 × 100 = 30 000 mm².
Total area = 10 000 + 30 000 = 40 000 mm².

11. E
A and D are both $^1/_{12}$.
B is $^3/_{12} + ^4/_{12} = ^7/_{12}$.
C is $^8/_{12} − ^3/_{12} = ^5/_{12}$.
E is $^3/_4$, which is the same as $^9/_{12}$.
This is larger than all the other fractions.

12. 1000 cm³
The width of each cube in cm is one more than the cube number. So the width of the 9th cube will be
9 + 1 = 10 cm.
Volume of a cube = width × width × width, so the 9th cube has a volume of 10 × 10 × 10 = 1000 cm³.

Test 10 — pages 30-32
1. D
The first, second and fourth shapes have five sides each, so they are pentagons. The third shape has six sides, so it is a hexagon. So option D is correct.

2. 10
The factors of 50 are: 1, 2, 5, 10, 25 and 50.
The factors of 60 are: 1, 2, 3, 4, 5, 6, 10, 12, 15, 20, 30 and 60. So the largest of the factors they have in common is 10.

3. £1.35
10% of £1.50 = £1.50 ÷ 10 = £0.15.
So the reduced price would be £1.50 − £0.15 = £1.35.

4. 121 cm²
The perimeter of a square is 4 × width, so the width of the square = 44 ÷ 4 = 11 cm.
The area of a square is width × width.
So the area = 11 × 11 = 121 cm².

5. B
The ruler shows that 5 cm is approximately 2 inches.
1 metre = 100 cm = 20 × 5 cm. So 1 metre is approximately 20 × 2 inches = 40 inches.

6. 180
The multiples of 10 below 200 are: 190, 180, 170...
190 is not a multiple of 9, but 180 is (180 = 9 × 20).
So 180 is the largest number under 200 that can be divided by both 9 or 10.

7. D
The people who own a pet are represented by half of a right angle (90°). So the number who own a pet must be half of $^1/_4$ of the total = $^1/_8$.
Half of these own a dog, so $^1/_8 ÷ 2 = ^1/_{16}$ own a dog.

8. 175
The fraction that do own a pet is $^1/_8$.
200 ÷ 8 = 25 people own a pet.
So 200 − 25 = 175 people do not own a pet.

9. 85 cm²
Add up the lengths of the grey rectangles to find the length of the blue rectangle: 3 + 8 + 6 = 17 cm.
The width of the blue rectangle is the same as the radius of the circle: 5 cm. Multiply the length by the width to find the area: 5 × 17 = 85 cm².

10. 81
The sequence is the squares of the odd numbers ($1^2, 3^2, 5^2, 7^2, ...$), so the next number will be $9^2 = 81$.

11. T
T has coordinates (3, 7),
so when $x = 3$, $y = 2 × 3 + 1 = 7$.
None of the other coordinates fit this pattern:
For S (3, 1), $x = 3$, so y would have to be 7, as above.
For U (5, 9), $x = 5$, so y would have to be 2 × 5 + 1 = 11.
For V (7, 3), $x = 7$, so y would have to be 2 × 7 + 1 = 15.
For W (9, 5), $x = 5$, so y would have to be 2 × 9 + 1 = 19.

12. E
For a translation of 2 squares left, the x-coordinate should decrease by 2, and for a translation of 1 square up, the y-coordinate should increase by 1.
So the coordinates of the translated point are
$(x − 2, 2x + 1 + 1) = (x − 2, 2x + 2)$.

Puzzles 2 — page 33
Safe as Houses
The correct code is 52691.

Interesting Times
The correct time is 16:01.

Test 11 — pages 34-36
1. D
30.5 cm is far too short to be the length of a netball court, and 30.5 mm is even shorter. 30.5 km is far too long. m² is a unit of area and not length. So the only possible length is 30.5 m (option D).

2. C
There are ten steps from 2.4 to 2.5. 2.5 − 2.4 = 0.1, so each step is worth 0.1 ÷ 10 = 0.01. The arrow is at the ninth step, so 0.01 × 9 = 0.09. This means the arrow is at 2.4 + 0.09 = 2.49.

3.   (2, 3)
If the ant turns 90° anticlockwise it will be facing west. Walking forwards two squares means the ant will move two squares to the left on the grid. So the x-coordinate of the ant's position, (4, 3), will decrease by 2 and the y-coordinate will stay the same: (2, 3).

4.   15 minutes
You need to find a number of minutes which is a multiple of 2.5 and 3. Since the number of minutes will be a multiple of 3, it will be a whole number. To get a whole number of minutes, Lisa will have to cycle around the track an even number of times. $2 \times 2.5 = 5$, so the number will also be a multiple of 5. The first number which is a multiple of 3 and 5 is 15. So they would next leave the start line at the same time at 15 minutes.

5.   D
The number of children that are 9 years old is $40 \div 5 = 8$. 15% of the children are 10 years old. 10% of 40 is 4 and 5% of 40 is 2, so 15% of 40 is $4 + 2 = 6$. So there are $8 + 6 = 14$ children that are 9 or 10 years old. This means that $40 - 14 = 26$ children are 11 years old.

6.   A
Divide the angle of the whole pie chart (360°) by 5.
$360° \div 5 = 72°$

7.   £17.91
4.5 kg of bird seed is the same as $4.5 \times 1000 = 4500$ g of bird seed. This means that $4500 \text{ g} \div 500 = 9$ bags of bird seed are needed. The price of 9 bags of bird seed ($9 \times £1.99$) can be worked out by multiplying by £2, then adjusting. $9 \times £2 = £18$. $£2 - £1.99 = 1$p, and $1\text{p} \times 9 = 9\text{p}$. $£18 - 9\text{p} = £17.91$.

8.   120 m²
The two long sides of the rectangle are $12 \text{ m} \times 2 = 24$ m in total. So the two shorter sides are $44 \text{ m} - 24 = 20$ m in total. One short side is $20 \text{ m} \div 2 = 10$ m. Area = length × width = $12 \text{ m} \times 10 \text{ m} = 120 \text{ m}^2$.

9.   230
Tom has £2 + £2 + 20p + 20p + 20p = £4.60 in total. £1 = 100p, so £4.60 = 460p. So he will receive $460\text{p} \div 2\text{p} = 230$ 2p coins.

10.   13 and 2
The prime numbers less than 20 are 2, 3, 5, 7, 11, 13, 17 and 19. Working backwards, $30 \div 2 = 15$, so the two numbers have to add up to 15. The only pair of prime numbers under 20 that add up to 15 are 13 and 2.

11.   C
Using the graph, baby Eric is 2.5 kg and baby Sue is about 7.75 pounds.
Sue is $3.5 - 2.5 = 1$ kg heavier than Eric so options A and B are false.
Sue is heavier than Eric by $7.75 - 5.5 = 2.25$ pounds, so options D and E are false and option C is true.

12.   62.8 cm
$C = 3.14d$ means the same as $C = 3.14 \times d$. Substitute 20 for d: $C = 3.14 \times 20$ is the same as $3.14 \times 2 \times 10 = 6.28 \times 10 = 62.8$ cm.

Test 12 — pages 37-39

1.   D
Six million is 6 000 000. Four hundred and thirty thousand is 430 000. Seventy-two is 72. Adding these together gives 6 430 072.

2.   32 km
25% = $^1/_4$, so the walk is $4 \times 8 = 32$ km.

3.   C
Read off the number of votes received by each act. Singer: 7 votes, gymnast: 3 votes, juggler: 14 votes, magician: 15 votes, dancer: 11 votes. Find two of the numbers which add together to make one of the other numbers: $3 + 11 = 14$. So the act with the same number of votes as two other acts combined is the juggler.

4.   5 : 1
The magician received 15 votes and the gymnast received 3 votes, so the ratio is 15 : 3. Divide both numbers by 3 to simplify the ratio: 5 : 1.

5.   4
List the numbers between 1 and 10 which are factors of 24: 1, 2, 3, 4, 6 and 8. Find which of these numbers are also factors of 30: 1, 2, 3 and 6. So 4 numbers on the spinner are factors of both 24 and 30.

6.   21
Each pattern in the sequence has 2 more lines than the pattern before. Pattern 10 is $10 - 4 = 6$ patterns after pattern 4 in the sequence. There are 9 lines in pattern 4, so pattern 10 will have $6 \times 2 = 12$ more lines: $9 + 12 = 21$ lines.

7.   58 hours
There are 24 hours in one day, so to 6 am on Wednesday there are $24 + 24 = 48$ hours. There are 6 hours to 12 pm on Wednesday, and then another 4 hours to 4 pm on Wednesday. So he has $48 + 6 + 4 = 58$ hours to complete the ride.

8.   34 km
To find the mean distance, divide the total distance by the number of hours: $136 \div 4$ (use partitioning). 136 km = 100 km + 36 km. $100 \div 4 = 25$ km, $36 \div 4 = 9$ km. So $136 \div 4 = 25 + 9 = 34$ km.

9.   B
Find how many times 8 km goes into 136 km. $136 \div 8 = 17$ (short division). Work out how many miles 136 km is approximately equal to by multiplying 5 miles by 17. $17 = 10 + 7$. $5 \times 10 = 50$, $5 \times 7 = 35$, so $5 \times 17 = 50 + 35 = 85$ miles (option B).

10.   4940 cm²
The floor measures 52 cm by 95 cm.
Area = length × width.

$$\begin{array}{r} 52 \\ \times\ 95 \\ \hline 260 \\ +4680 \\ \hline 4940 \end{array}$$

11.   D
100 cm = 1 m, so 95 cm = 0.95 m, 141 cm = 1.41 m, 52 cm = 0.52 m. Round each measurement to a sensible value. 0.95 m rounds to 1 m. 1.41 m rounds to 1.4 m. 0.52 m rounds to 0.5 m. Estimate the volume of the cage using these values: $1 \times 1.4 \times 0.5 = 0.7 \text{ m}^3$. Work out how many rats could be kept in the cage by dividing the whole volume by the volume needed for one rat: $0.7 \div 0.07 = 10$ rats.

12. A
The *y*-coordinate is always half of the *x*-coordinate at any point on the graph. So $y = \frac{1}{2}x$ (option A).

Test 13 — pages 40-42
1. 2
To make the grid symmetrical in both lines of symmetry, 2 squares need to be shaded.

2. C
There are two pairs of equal angles in a parallelogram so option A and E are incorrect. The angles must add up to 360°: 50 + 50 + 125 + 125 = 350° (option B) and 50 + 50 + 40 + 40 = 180° (option D), so option C must be correct, since 50 + 50 + 130 + 130 = 360°.

3. C
The height of 100 new pound coins is 100 × 2.8 = 280 mm. The height of 100 old pound coins is 100 × 3.15 = 315 mm. The difference in height between the two towers is 315 − 280 = 35 mm. 10 mm = 1 cm, so 35 mm = 3.5 cm. So option C is correct.

4. 12.9 cm
The length of the model will be 15% of 86 cm. 10% of 86 cm is 86 ÷ 10 = 8.6 cm. 5% of 86 cm is 8.6 cm ÷ 2 = 4.3 cm. So 15% is 10% + 5% = 8.6 + 4.3 = 12.9 cm.

5. 160 cm²
The base of one triangle is 32 cm ÷ 2 = 16 cm.
The height of one triangle is 20 cm.
Area of a triangle = $\frac{1}{2}$ × base × height
= $\frac{1}{2}$ × 16 × 20 = 8 × 20 = 160 cm².

6. 25%
There are two smaller right-angled triangles left over on each side of the piece of card. Each left over triangle is equivalent to half of one of the blue triangles, so together they have the area of one blue triangle. This means the total area of piece of card is the same as the area of 4 triangles, so $\frac{1}{4}$ of the card is wasted which is equivalent to 25%.

7. £79.92
Multiply the cost per litre of petrol by the number of litres in a full tank using partitioning.
£1.11 = £1 + 10p + 1p.
£1 × 72 = £72, 10p × 72 = 720p = £7.20, 1p × 72 = 72p. So £1.11 × 72 = £72 + £7.20 + 72p = £79.92.

8. 45 litres
There are 8 intervals between an empty tank and a full tank, so each interval shows $\frac{1}{8}$ of the petrol in a full tank. $\frac{1}{8}$ of the petrol in a full tank is 72 ÷ 8 = 9 litres. The arrow points to the mark after the fifth interval, so there are 5 × $\frac{1}{8}$ = $\frac{5}{8}$ of the petrol left.
So there are 5 × 9 = 45 litres of petrol left in the tank.

9. B
Each interval on the *y*-axis = 100 ÷ 4 = 25 books. Between the ends of week 1 and week 2, the graph increases by 2 intervals, so there were 2 × 25 = 50 books read during the second week.

10. 10
The graph shows that 300 books were read in the first four weeks of the readathon. To find the mean number of books, divide the total number of books by the number of children: 300 ÷ 30 = 10 books.

11. C
Divide both sides of the equation by 3:
3(*x* − 2) ÷ 3 = 39 ÷ 3
x − 2 = 13
Add 2 to both sides of the equation: *x* = 13 + 2 = 15.

12. C
Multiplying any number by an even number will always produce an even number, so option A will always produce even numbers and options B and E will produce even numbers if *n* is an even number. Adding 2 to an even number will always produce an even number, so option D is incorrect. Adding 1 to an even number will always produce an odd number, so option C is correct.

Test 14 — pages 43-45
1. 6
Find the number of brothers by working out how many times £30 goes into £180. 18 ÷ 3 = 6, so 180 ÷ 30 = 6.

2. E
Work out which faces are opposite when folded into a cube:
So option E will be the face at the bottom.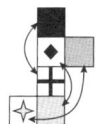

3. A
Count back in 3s from 17 until you reach a negative number: 17, 14, 11, 8, 5, 2, −1. So −1 is the first number below zero that Karen will count.

4. C
1000 ml = 1 litre, so 500 ml = 0.5 litres and 150 ml = 0.15 litres. Ahmed makes 1.75 + 0.5 = 2.25 litres of fizzy apple juice. After drinking some of the mixture, there is 2.25 − 0.15 = 2.1 litres left in the jug.

5. 60
Count the number of children who have lost 7 or more teeth: 20 + 21 + 19 = 60 children.

6. B
Add up how many children were asked in total using chunking: 30 + 25 + 35 = 90. 20 + 21 + 19 = 60. So there were 90 + 60 = 150 children in total. 30 out of 150, or $\frac{30}{150}$, children hadn't lost any teeth. Divide the top and bottom of the fraction by 30 to simplify the fraction: $\frac{1}{5}$.

7. 50 ml
There are 1 + 5 = 6 parts paint in total. So each part is 300 ÷ 6 = 50 ml. So Kay should use 50 ml of blue paint.

8. 1.025 kg
The mass of 100 pound coins is 100 × 9.5 = 950 g. So the total mass of the money box and coins is 75 + 950 = 1025 g. 1000 g = 1 kg, so 1025 g = 1.025 kg.

9. 11:10 am
60 secs = 1 min, so 90 secs = 1.5 mins.
1 set of running and walking lasts 1.5 + 2 = 3.5 mins. So six sets of walking and running is 6 × 3.5 mins. 6 × 3 = 18 mins. 6 × 0.5 = 3 mins, so 6 × 3.5 = 18 + 3 = 21 mins. 21 mins = 11 mins + 10 mins. 11 mins after 10:49 is 11:00 am. 10 mins after 11:00 am is 11:10 am.

10. 23.2 m
Volume = length × width × height
348 = length × 5 × 3
348 = length × 15.
So length = 348 ÷ 15:

```
     23.2
15)348.0
    30↓
    48
    45↓
     30
     30
      0
```

11. C
Point (4, 9) has been translated 3 units to the right (7 − 4 = 3), so the x-coordinate of point P will be 3 units bigger: 6 + 3 = 9. Point (4, 9) has moved 1 unit down (9 − 8 = 1), so the y-coordinate of point P will be 1 unit smaller: 3 − 1 = 2. The coordinates of point P are (9, 2).

12. £68.00
Substitute 20 for m in the formula: $C = 50 + (0.9 \times 20)$.
0.9 × 10 = 9, so 0.9 × 20 = 9 × 2 = 18.
C = 50 + 18 = £68.00

Test 15 — pages 46-48
1. 97 minutes
Work out how long it takes the bus to get from Easton to Fryton using chunking. At 10:00 it has travelled for 33 minutes. At 11:00 it has travelled a further 60 minutes. At 11:04 it has travelled another 4 minutes. So it takes the bus 33 + 60 + 4 = 97 minutes.

2. 0.67
To find the largest and smallest numbers, look at the digits in each column of the numbers, from left to right. Each number has 8 in the tens column. 88.10 and 88.04 both have 8 in the ones column but 88.10 has a higher number in the tenths column, so it's the largest. 87.43 and 87.62 both have 7 in the ones column but 87.43 has a lower number in the tenths column, so it's the smallest.
The difference between the numbers is 88.10 − 87.43. Use partitioning: 87.43 = 87 + 0.4 + 0.03.
88.10 − 87 = 1.10, 1.1 − 0.4 = 0.7, 0.7 − 0.03 = 0.67.

3. B
Angle x is bigger than 180° so it can't be options A or C. 181° is almost a straight line, so option E is incorrect. 260° is almost a right angle (90°) bigger than a straight line (180°), which is too big, so option D must be incorrect. So the best estimate of angle x must be 200° (option B).

4. D
(2 − 1) × 4 = 1 × 4 = 4. (4 − 1) × 4 = 3 × 4 = 12.
Clive's sequence is option D.

5. B
The total of the ages of the children is 5 + 6 + 8 + 2 + 4 + 5 = 30. So the mean age is the total age divided by the number of children: 30 ÷ 6 = 5.

6. 2 and 4
The total age of all the children is 30 (worked out in previous answer). The total age of the girls is 4 × 6 = 24. So the sum of the ages of the two boys is 30 − 24 = 6. Find two of the ages which add to 6. The boys must be 2 and 4.

7. 134
Work out how many times 9 goes into 1204:
```
   133 r7
 9)1204
```
So Jo will need 134 boxes to pack away all the baubles.

8. 115
The 23 blue cars make up $1/8$ of the total number of cars. The number of red cars is $1/4 = 2/8$ of the total number of cars. So the number of silver cars is $8/8 − 2/8 − 1/8 = 5/8$ of the total number of cars. So there were 5 × 23 silver cars. Use partitioning: 23 = 20 + 3: 5 × 20 = 100, 5 × 3 = 15, so there were 100 + 15 = 115 silver cars.

9. D
138 × 4.4 will be 10 times smaller than 138 × 44.
6072 ÷ 100 will be 100 times smaller than 6072.
So the two sides of the calculation in option D are not equal.

10. £28.08
10% of £48 is 48 ÷ 10 = £4.80.
30% of £48 is £4.80 × 3 = £14.40 (use partitioning).
5% of £48 is £4.80 ÷ 2 = £2.40.
So 35% of £48 is £14.40 + £2.40 = £16.80. So the sale price is £48 − £16.80:
£48 − £16 = £32, £32 − £0.80 = £31.20
10% of £31.20 is £3.12.
So Ryan pays £31.20 − £3.12:
£31.20 − £3 = £28.20, £28.20 − £0.12 = £28.08.

11. 43
Find the multiples of 7 between 30 and 50: 35, 42, 49. Add 1 to each number: 36, 43, 50. 36 and 50 are both multiples of 2, so the prime number must be 43.

12. C
A kite has two pairs of equal sides, so its perimeter will be $6 + 6 + x + 3 + x + 3 = 2x + 18$.

Puzzles 3 — page 49
Cake Cutting
Clare ate the 30° slice, Dillon ate the 90° slice, Adam ate the 120° slice, Gosia ate the 60° slice, Fred ate the smallest slice (10°), Eve ate the 50° slice.

Symbol Sums
△ = 3 ◇ = 6 ▢ = 9 ⇧ = 5
✶ = 7 ♥ = 4 ☆ = 8 ⬇ = 2

Test 16 — pages 50-52
1. 6
30 + 30 + 30 = 90, and 6 × 15 = 90.

2. 88 minutes
0931 to 1031 is 1 hour = 60 minutes.
1031 to 1059 is 28 minutes.
So total time = 60 + 28 = 88 minutes.
(It is the same time for each train on the timetable.)

3. 09:46
To get to Mancton by noon, the latest train she can get is the 1031 train from Birville (which arrives in Mancton at 1159). She needs to leave the house $3/4$ of an hour = 45 minutes before 1031, which is 09:46 (minus 1 hour and plus 15 mins).

4. C
A is false because a square is a regular quadrilateral. B, D and E are false because their diagonals are not lines of symmetry.

5. £1.60
£2.00 + £1.00 + £1.50 + £2.25 + £1.25 = £8.00.
£8.00 ÷ 5 days = £1.60 (use short division).

6.   C
$^{18}/_8 = {}^{(16+2)}/_8 = {}^{16}/_8 + {}^2/_8 = 2 + {}^2/_8 = 2{}^1/_4$
$^1/_4$ is equivalent to 0.25, so $2{}^1/_4 = 2.25$.

7.   C
There are $96 \div 4 = 24$ raisins, so in total there are $96 + 24 = 120$ nuts and raisins.

8.   27 cm²
The front and back faces each have an area of $2 \times 3 = 6$ cm². The side faces each have an area of $2 \times 1.5 = 3$ cm². The top and bottom faces each have an area of $3 \times 1.5 = 4.5$ cm². So the total area of the net is: $(2 \times 6) + (2 \times 3) + (2 \times 4.5) = 12 + 6 + 9 = 27$ cm².

9.   D
Even though the top section for 'cherry' represents 10%, the area of the bar is smaller than a 10% section would be lower down the jar.

10.   A
The 'raspberry' section represents $90 - 50 = 40\%$ of the total number of jars of jam. 10% of 90 = 9 jars, so 40% of 90 = $4 \times 9 = 36$ jars.

11.   £2.05
Half an hour = 30 minutes, so $m = 30$.
$C = 25 + (6 \times 30) = 25 + 180 = 205\text{p} = £2.05$

12.   19:52
$85 = 25 + 6m$, so $6m = 60$, and so $m = 10$ minutes.
The call started 10 minutes before 20:02, which is 19:52.

Test 17 — pages 53-55
1.   72
There are only two multiples of 9 between 60 and 80 — these are 63 and 72. Only 72 is also a multiple of 4.

2.   D
4.5 litres = 4.5×1.8 pints, which is approximately, but a little less than, $4.5 \times 2 = 9$ pints.
So 8 is the closest option.

3.   30
4.5 litres × 1000 = 4500 ml.
$4500 \div 150 = 450 \div 15 = 30$ (it is 10 times bigger than $45 \div 15 = 3$). So he can fill 30 cups.

4.   2
The terms in the sequence decrease by 3 each time, so to find the first term, add on 3 twice to –4.
Second term = $-4 + 3 = -1$
First term = $-1 + 3 = 2$

5.   E
Options A-D are equal to 27.
$^2/_7$ of 10 is $^{20}/_7$, which is equal to $2{}^6/_7$.

6.   C
$12345 \div 100 = 123.45$
$12.345 \times 100 = 1234.5$
So the two sides of the equation are not equal if both boxes contain 100.

7.   D
Thirty-two thousand five hundred is 32 500.
The largest number the population could be is 32 549. If it was 32 550, it would round up to 32 600.

8.   2.2 °C

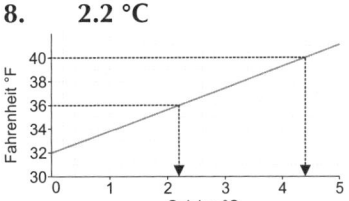

From the graph:
36 °F is 2.2 °C, 40 °F is 4.4 °C
So the difference in temperature is $4.4 - 2.2 = 2.2$ °C.

9.   E
1 m = 100 cm, so 0.01 m = 1 cm.
The radius is half of the diameter, so radius = 0.5 cm.
1 cm = 10 mm, so 0.5 cm = 5 mm.

10.   90°
The shopkeeper sell $50 - 20 = 30$ meat pies, and 20 vegetable pies.
Amount of money from vegetable pies = $20 \times £1.50 = £30$.
Amount of money from meat pies = $30 \times £3.00 = £90$.
Total made = $£30 + £90 = £120$, of which $^{30}/_{120}$ comes from the vegetable pies. Simplify $^{30}/_{120}$ by dividing the top and bottom by 30 to get $^1/_4$.
$^1/_4$ of 360° = 90°, so the shopkeeper should use 90° for the section representing the money made from selling vegetable pies.

11.   8 cm³
The sheet of paper measures 3 squares by 4 squares. So the paper could be divided into $3 \times 4 = 12$ squares. The area of the paper is 48 cm² so each square has an area of $48 \div 12 = 4$ cm². So each side of each square must be 2 cm ($2 \times 2 = 4$ cm²). So the volume of the cube will be $2 \times 2 \times 2 = 8$ cm³.

12.   C
The angles in a triangle add up to 180°, which gives:
$2y + 6y - 10° + 4y + 10° = 180°$
$12y - 10° + 10° = 180°$
$12y = 180°$ (so options A, B and D must be incorrect).
Dividing both sides of the equation by 2 gives:
$6y = 90°$ (so option E must be incorrect).

Test 18 — pages 56-58
1.   3
There are 5 faces in total — two triangular ends and three rectangles.

2.   11
Customers with a cat but no dog = $57 - 26 = 31$.
Customers with no dog and no cat = $42 - 31 = 11$.

3.   58%
Customers with a dog = $100 - 42 = 58$.
There are 100 customers in total, so $^{58}/_{100} = 58\%$ own a dog.

4.   D
Plot the point $(-1, -3)$ on the grid. Its reflection in the vertical y-axis has the same coordinates as point D:

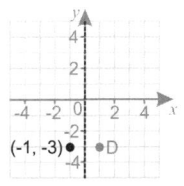

5.   D
If the mean length (in cm) of the four pieces of string is 10, then the lengths must add up to 4 × 10 = 40. So 7, 11 and 23 could not be three of these lengths, because they add up to 41, which is too big even without the fourth length. All the other options add up to less than 40, so they could possibly be three of the four lengths.

6.   0.7
$1/2$ is equivalent to 0.5 and $4/5$ is equivalent to 0.8. So $4\tfrac{1}{2} - 3\tfrac{4}{5}$ is the same as 4.5 − 3.8, which is 0.7.

7.   100
There are 5 child symbols and 17.5 adult symbols, so there are 17.5 − 5 = 12.5 more adult symbols than child symbols. 12.5 symbols represents 1250 people. 12.5 × 100 = 1250, so 1 symbol represents 100 people.

8.   C
Opposite angles in a parallelogram are equal, and all four angles add to 360°. So, $2x + x + 2x + x = 360°$. $6x = 360°$. So x must be 60° (divide both sides by 6).

9.   2.4 kg
320 g serves 4 people, so 320 g ÷ 4 = 80 g serves 1 person, and 30 × 80 g = 2400 g serves 30 people. 1000 g = 1 kg, so 2400 g = 2.4 kg.

10.   C
If only 24 people are served, then 30 − 24 = 6 people's rice will be wasted. This is $6/30 = 2/10 = 20\%$.

11.   6241 mm²
The area of the parallelogram equals the area of the square. The square's sides measure 316 ÷ 4 = 79 mm. Area = 79 × 79 = 6241 mm² (using long multiplication).

12.   E
In each shape, the height of the rectangle is n cm, and the width is $3n$ cm. So the perimeter of each rectangle is $n + 3n + n + 3n = 8n$. None of the other options simplify to this.

Test 19 — pages 59-61
1.   123 500
The digit in the column to the right of the hundreds column is 5, so the 4 in the hundreds column rounds up to 500.

2.   B
There are 7 squares between point Y and point Z. So the mirror line must be halfway between them: 7 ÷ 2 = 3.5, so the mirror line is 3.5 squares right of point Y.

3.   E
The sequence in E increases each term by 9, so the seventh term is 44 + 9 + 9 = 62. This is the only option that does not have 64 as a seventh term. The sequence in A doubles each term to get the next term, so the seventh term is 16 × 2 × 2 = 64. The sequence in B increases each term by 5, so the seventh term is 54 + 5 + 5 = 64. The sequence in C is the square numbers, starting with 2^2. So the seventh term is $8^2 = 64$. The sequence in D decreases each term by 6, so the seventh term is 76 − 6 − 6 = 64.

4.   6
The two prime numbers between 60 and 70 are 61 and 67. 67 − 61 = 6.

5.   D
Using the information in the question, the scale can be completed on the graph as follows:

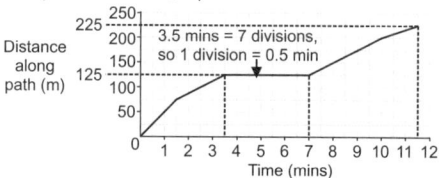

The graph shows that she walked 225 m in total, so option D is true. A is false because the graph shows she stopped after 3.5 minutes. B is false because the graph shows she walked 225 − 125 = 100 m after she stopped. C is false because the graph shows she reached the end of the path after 11.5 minutes. E is false because the graph shows she walked for 11.5 − 7 = 4.5 minutes after she stopped.

6.   12:44
Rose reached the end of the path after 11.5 minutes, so she finished the whole walk in 11.5 × 2 = 23 minutes. She must have started the walk 23 minutes before 13:07, which is 16 minutes (23 − 7) before 13:00, which is 12:44.

7.   C
$1/4$ is equivalent to $3/12$. $7/12 + 3/12 = 10/12 = 5/6$ of the coins are not 50p coins. This leaves $1/6$ of the coins which are 50p coins.

8.   £4.60
$7/12 = 14/24$, so there are 14 × 10p coins, worth £1.40. $1/4 = 6/24$, so there are 6 × 20p coins, worth £1.20. There are 24 − 14 − 6 = 4 × 50p coins, worth £2.00. So Jay has £1.40 + £1.20 + £2.00 = £4.60.

9.   C
1 m = 100 cm, so the track is 14.3 × 100 = 1430 cm long. The number of hops × 65 = 1430. 10 × 60 = 650 (too small), and 100 × 65 = 6500 (too big), so the number of hops must be between 10 and 100. 22 is the only option in this range.

10.   29 seconds
The carrot is pulled a distance of 0.5 m in 1 s, so it will be pulled a distance of 1 m in 2 s, and 14.3 m in 14.3 × 2 = 28.6 s. This rounds to 29 s, to the nearest second.

11.   8
41 − 3h = 17, so 3h = 41 − 17 = 24. 3h = 24 so h = 24 ÷ 3 = 8.

12.   45
The 'Easy' and 'Medium' sectors make up $3/4$ of the pie in total. $3/4$ of 80 cyclists = (80 ÷ 4) × 3 = 60 cyclists. So $3a + a = 4a = 60$ cyclists. This means that $a = 60 ÷ 4 = 15$ cyclists, and so $3a$ (the 'Easy' sector angle) = 3 × 15 = 45 cyclists.

Test 20 — pages 62-64
1.   C
Twenty-seven pounds = £27. C is correct because −8 + 27 = 19. A is incorrect because −5 + 27 = 22, not 32. B is incorrect because −7 + 27 = 20, not 21. D and E are both incorrect because −9 + 27 = 18, not 19 or 17.

2. 60 m³
The volume of a cuboid is length × width × height.
So volume = 4 × 2.5 × 6 = 10 × 6 = 60 m³.

3. E
Work out $\frac{1}{5}$ of $\frac{1}{3}$: $\frac{1}{3} \div 5 = \frac{1}{15}$.

4. 135°
An octagon has 8 angles, so the size of each angle must be 1080° ÷ 8 = 135° (use short division).

5. B
The vertical scale on the graph has 5 divisions for every 10 pupils, so each division = 10 ÷ 5 = 2 pupils. Reading off the graph, the heights of the bars are:
0 pets = 12 pupils. 1 pet = 19 pupils. 2 pets = 9 pupils.
3 pets = 6 pupils. 4 pets = 2 pupils. The total number of pupils is 12 + 19 + 9 + 6 + 2 = 48. 6 + 2 = 8 of these have at least 3 pets. So the fraction is $\frac{8}{48} = \frac{1}{6}$ (simplify by dividing top and bottom by 8).

6. 63
19 pupils have 1 pet = 19 pets
9 pupils have 2 pets = 9 × 2 = 18 pets
6 pupils have 3 pets = 6 × 3 = 18 pets
2 pupils have 4 pets = 2 × 4 = 8 pets
So there are 19 + 18 + 18 + 8 = 63 pets in total.

7. 7
There are 8 × 20 = 160 squares in total.
Using short division to share 160 between 9 gives:
   1 7 r7
9 ⟌ 1 6⁷0   So there are 7 squares left over.

8. £3.23
10% of £3.80 = £3.80 ÷ 10 = £0.38
5% of £3.80 = £0.38 ÷ 2 = £0.19
So 15% of £3.80 = £0.38 + £0.19 = £0.57.
The reduced price is £3.80 − £0.57 = £3.23.

9. 1.53 m
100 cm = 1 m, so 125 cm = 1.25 m, 162 cm = 1.62 m.
The total of the four heights is:
1.55 + 1.25 + 1.7 + 1.62 = 6.12 m.
To find the mean, use short division to divide 6.12 by 4:
   1. 5 3
4 ⟌ 6. ²1 ¹2   So the mean height is 1.53 m.

10. B
The shortest person in the group is 125 cm tall.
If 1 inch = 2.5 cm, then 10 inches = 25 cm. There are 5 lots of 25 in 125, so 125 cm = 5 × 10 = 50 inches.
There are 12 inches in a foot, so this means
50 inches = (4 × 12) + 2 inches = 4 feet 2 inches.

11. E
The area of the square is $a \times a$ or a^2, so this rules out options A and C.
The area of the rectangle is $b \times (b + 5)$, which can be written as both $b(b + 5)$ and $b(5 + b)$, so this rules out options B and D. $b(b + 5)$ can't be written as $2b + 5$.

12. 4 cm
The area of the square = 6 × 6 = 36 cm². This is the same as the area of the rectangle, so the length (b) and width ($b + 5$) of the rectangle must multiply together to make 36, and have a difference of 5.
b is a whole number, so find the factor pairs of 36:
1 and 36, 2 and 18, 3 and 12, 4 and 9, 6 and 6.
The only pair with a difference of 5 is 4 and 9, so length b must be 4 cm (and $b + 5 = 9$ cm).

Puzzles 4 — page 65
In a Pickle
The sugar is the ingredient that will run out first.
She has 1000 g of sugar, which means she can make 8 lots of the recipe, using: 64 limes, 24 garlic cloves and 64 cm³ of ginger. This leaves: 16 limes, 12 garlic cloves and 56 cm³ of ginger.

Riddle Me This
Its name is CROAKY.

Test 21 — pages 66-68
1. 80
Use partitioning to subtract 75 from 155:
155 − 75 = 155 − 55 − 20 = 100 − 20 = 80.

2. 18 minutes
1 hour = 60 minutes, so 2 hours = 2 × 60 = 120 minutes. Use partitioning to work out 15% of 120:
10% of 120 is 120 ÷ 10 = 12 minutes.
5% is 12 ÷ 2 = 6 minutes.
So 15% is 12 + 6 = 18 minutes.

3. 21 minutes
The time on the clock reads 9 minutes past 4. Convert this to the 24 hour clock: 16:09. It is 12 minutes from 15:48 to 16:00, then 9 minutes from 16:00 to 16:09.
So it took Jackson 12 + 9 = 21 minutes to get home.

4. E
Change the fractions so that they have the same denominator:
Multiply the top and bottom of $\frac{1}{4}$ by 5 to give $\frac{5}{20}$.
Multiply the top and bottom of $\frac{2}{5}$ by 4 to give $\frac{8}{20}$.
Add the fractions together to give $\frac{5}{20} + \frac{8}{20} = \frac{13}{20}$.

5. B
B is correct because 5 × 11 = 55, minus 7 = 48, which rounds to 50. A is incorrect because 5 × 9 = 45, minus 7 = 38, which rounds to 40. C is incorrect because 7 × 9 = 63, minus 7 = 56, which rounds to 60. D is incorrect because 7 × 11 = 77, minus 7 = 70.
E is incorrect because 9 × 11 = 99, minus 7 = 92, which rounds to 90.

6. 147
Add together all the numbers in the tennis circle of the Venn diagram: 34 + 17 + 54 + 42 = 147.

7. 81
Add together all the numbers that are not in the football circle of the Venn diagram: 17 + 42 + 22 = 81.

8. £2.10
Benji spends
£2.40 + £0.90 + £0.90 + £0.55 + £0.55 = £5.30.
So Benji has £7.40 − £5.30 = £2.10 left.

9. 0.5 km
15 minutes is a quarter of an hour. In 15 minutes Skyla runs 10 ÷ 4 = 2.5 km and Paloma runs 12 ÷ 4 = 3 km.
So Paloma runs 3 − 2.5 = 0.5 km further than Skyla.

10.   C
Work out which direction she is facing after each turn.

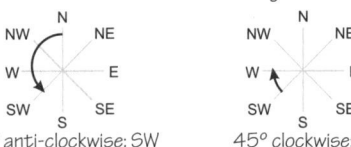

135° anti-clockwise: SW   45° clockwise: W

11.   C
Work out the height of each triangle using the formula:
height = area ÷ ($\frac{1}{2}$ × base).
Option A: height = 21 ÷ ($\frac{1}{2}$ × 6) = 21 ÷ 3 = 7 cm
Option B: height = 20 ÷ ($\frac{1}{2}$ × 5) = 20 ÷ 2.5 = 8 cm
Option C: height = 15 ÷ ($\frac{1}{2}$ × 3) = 15 ÷ 1.5 = 10 cm
Option D: height = 8 ÷ ($\frac{1}{2}$ × 8) = 8 ÷ 4 = 2 cm
Option E: height = 12 ÷ ($\frac{1}{2}$ × 4) = 12 ÷ 2 = 6 cm
So option C is the tallest.

12.   30
Work out the total of the unknown angles by subtracting the known angles from 360°: 360 − 90 − 120 = 150.
So 150 = 2a + 2a + a = 5a. So a = 150 ÷ 5 = 30.

Test 22 — pages 69-71

1.   B
Convert all the prices to the same unit. 100p = £1, so 45p = £0.45. Order the prices in £ from smallest to largest: £0.45, £0.54, £4.05, £4.50, £5.40.
So from smallest to largest the prices are:
45p, £0.54, £4.05, £4.50, £5.40.

2.   12 cm
1 m = 100 cm. After cutting off 4 cm of ribbon, she has 100 − 4 = 96 cm of ribbon remaining. So each length of ribbon that she cuts will be 96 ÷ 8 = 12 cm long.

3.   C
The numbers in the grey box need to be odd and multiples of 7. Only option C has numbers which are all odd and multiples of 7: 21, 35, 77.

4.   A
$\frac{3}{5}$ is equivalent to $\frac{12}{20}$, so option A ($\frac{13}{20}$) is bigger.

5.   13 mm
Work out the length of each car by finding the difference between the ruler measurements at each end of the car.
Car A: 6.1 cm − 0.5 cm = 5.6 cm.
Car B: 11.6 cm − 7.3 cm = 4.3 cm.
Work out the difference between the two car lengths:
5.6 cm − 4.3 cm = 1.3 cm.
1 cm = 10 mm, so 1.3 cm × 10 = 13 mm

6.   D
After the reflection, the shape looks like this:

7.   B
The pie chart shows that $\frac{1}{2}$ of the pupils have blue eyes and $\frac{1}{4}$ of the pupils have brown eyes.
So 72 ÷ 2 = 36 pupils have blue eyes and 72 ÷ 4 = 18 pupils have brown eyes. So the number of pupils with green eyes is 72 − 6 − 36 − 18 = 12 pupils.

8.   150 g
The jar contains 23% + 47% = 70% red and blue jelly beans.
So 100% − 70% = 30% of the jelly beans are green. 30% of 100 g is 30 g, so 30% of 500 g is 30 g × 5 = 150 g.

9.   C
Sanjit has m + 4 packs of stickers. So in total they have m + m + 4 = 2m + 4 packs of stickers.

10.   10
The number of packs of stickers bought = 2m + 4 (found in the previous question), so 2m + 4 = 16.
So 2m must be equal to 16 − 4 = 12, and m must be equal to 12 ÷ 2 = 6.
Sanjit has m + 4 packs of stickers = 6 + 4 = 10.

11.   1.76 litres
Carlton has 2 more symbols than Casey on the pictogram. Each symbol stands for 4 cups, so Carlton has sold 4 × 2 = 8 more cups than Casey.
Each cup contains 220 ml of lemonade, so Carlton has sold 8 × 220 ml = 1760 ml more lemonade than Casey (use partitioning).
1000 ml = 1 litre, so 1760 ml ÷ 1000 = 1.76 litres.

12.   £68.10
The total number of symbols in the pictogram is 17.5.
So the total number of cups sold is 17.5 × 4 = 70.
The total made from selling the lemonade is
70 × £1.20 = £84.00 (use partitioning).
So the profit made is £84.00 − £15.90 = £68.10.

Test 23 — pages 72-74

1.   B
To work out the missing value, divide 3640 by 100:
3640 ÷ 100 = 36.4

2.   C
Chapter 1 is 30 pages long.
Chapter 2 is 75 − 30 = 45 pages long.
Chapter 3 is 133 − 75 = 58 pages long.
Chapter 4 is 184 − 133 = 51 pages long.
Chapter 5 is 227 − 184 = 43 pages long.
So chapter 3 is the longest.

3.   C
An acute angle is smaller than a right angle.
So Angles d and g are acute. All of the other labelled angles are bigger than a right angle.

4.   134°
The angles on a straight line add up to 180°.
So angle h is 180° − 46° = 134°.

5.   81
Work out how many sets of 2 steps John takes:
54 ÷ 2 = 27. Robyn takes 3 steps for every 2 of John's, so she must have taken 27 × 3 = 81 steps.

6.   £0.10
One beef burger costs £4.20 ÷ 6 = £0.70.
One lamb burger costs £3.00 ÷ 5 = £0.60.
So one beef burger costs £0.70 − £0.60 = £0.10 more than one lamb burger.

7.   10:55 am
Each line on the timeline is equal to 15 minutes.
Read off the timeline that Giovanna has lunch at 12:15.
Use partitioning (1 hour 20 mins = 1 hour + 15 mins + 5 mins) to work out what time she goes to the park.
12:15 minus 1 hour is 11:15, minus 15 minutes is 11:00, minus 5 minutes is 10:55.

8. 1 hour 10 mins
Add on the length of each activity to 12:15:
12:15 + 25 mins = 12:40. 12:40 + 1 hour = 1:40.
1:40 + 30 mins = 2:10.
1 hour 55 mins = 2 hours minus 5 mins.
So, 2:10 + 2 hours = 4:10, minus 5 mins = 4:05.
The timeline shows dinner time is at 5:15, so she has to wait 1 hour and 10 mins.

9. E
The x-coordinate of the point must be between −60 and 20. The y-coordinate must be between −30 and 20. So only option E (−41, 6) will be inside the rectangle.

10. C
Round 342.6 and 1393.8 to the nearest 10 to give 340 and 1390. Find the difference between 340 and 1390: 1390 − 340 = 1050. Divide 1050 by 2 to give 525. Add 525 to 340 to find the approximate halfway point: 525 + 340 = 865. So find the option closest to 865. The answer must be option C.

11. 1899
Add up the number of competitors in each points group to work out the number of competitors in total:
4 + 7 + 11 + 5 + 3 = 30. Multiply the number of competitors by the mean number of points to find the total number of points: 30 × 63.3 = 1899 (which is the same as 3 × 633 — use partitioning).

12. D
3 people scored 80-89 points and 5 people scored 70-79 points, so 3 + 5 = 8 people scored 70 or more points. 11 people scored 60-69 points, so 8 + 11 = 19 people scored 60 or more points. So the person in 15th place scored between 60 and 69 points. So only option D could have been the number of points scored by the person in 15th place, as 69 is the only value in this range.

Test 24 — pages 75-77

1. 2
The factors of 36 between 10 and 20 are 12 and 18.

2. D
Option A has a difference of 1.66 − 1.24 = 0.42.
Option B has a difference of 0.38 − 0.31 = 0.07.
Option C has a difference of 4.7 − 1.0 = 3.7.
Option D has a difference of 5.18 − 4.81 = 0.37.
Option E has a difference of 9.58 − 9.22 = 0.36.

3. 100 g
The recipe uses 150 ÷ 75 = 2 times the amount of chocolate as butter. So Eliza will need to use 50 × 2 = 100 g of chocolate.

4. 12
Eliza has $^{50}/_{75}$ of the butter needed for the recipe. Simplify the fraction by dividing the top and bottom by 25: $^{2}/_{3}$. So Eliza will be able to make $^{2}/_{3}$ of the 18 cakes. $^{1}/_{3}$ of the cakes would be 18 ÷ 3 = 6 cakes.
So Eliza can make 2 × 6 = 12 cakes.

5. A
Trapeziums do not have 2 pairs of equal parallel sides. All sides of a rhombus and a square are the same length. A rectangle only has right angles. Only a parallelogram has all of the features that Zoe describes.

6. 69
Work out what each part of the sum is equal to:
$2^3 = 8$, $3^2 = 9$, $3^3 = 27$, $5^2 = 25$.
Find the sum of the parts: 8 + 9 + 27 + 25 = 69.

7. D
Work out which faces of the net will be opposite each other when folded into a cube. Find the net where the numbers on each pair of opposite faces adds up to 7.
Callum must use option D.

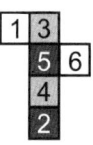

8. D
The kite has a vertical line of symmetry, so the two smaller sides are both 2.6 cm, and the two longer sides are both 3.9 cm. So the perimeter of the kite shown is 2.6 + 2.6 + 3.9 + 3.9 = 13 cm.
So the perimeter of the enlarged kite is
2.5 × 13 = (2 × 13) + (0.5 × 13) = 26 + 6.5 = 32.5 cm.

9. 22
There were 2 adults per family ticket, so on Monday there were 19 + (2 × 7) = 19 + 14 = 33 adults that saw the film. On Friday there were 33 + (2 × 11) = 33 + 22 = 55 adults that saw the film. So 55 − 33 = 22 more adults saw than film on Friday than on Monday.

10. £301
The adult tickets made 13 × £10 = £130.
The child tickets made 16 × £6 = £96.
The family tickets made 3 × £25 = £75.
So in total the cinema made 130 + 96 + 75 = £301.

11. C
Half of the tickets sold were child tickets, so the pie chart can't be for Monday or Friday. There were more than twice as many adult tickets sold as family tickets, so the pie chart can't be for Tuesday. There were less than three times as many adult tickets sold as family tickets, so the pie chart can't be for Thursday. So the pie chart shows Wednesday's ticket sales.

12. C
Put $x = 7$ and $y = 3$ into each expression.
Option A: (6 × 7) + (12 × 3) = 42 + 36 = 78
Option B: (7 × 7) + 3^2 + 15 = 49 + 9 + 15 = 73
Option C: 4 × 7 × 3 = 84
Option D: 7^2 + (4 × 3) − (7 × 3) = 49 + 12 − 21 = 40
Option E: (5 × 7 × 3) − 10 = 95
So Marley's expression is option C.

Test 25 — pages 78-80

1. 80
56 ÷ 7 = 8 (using multiplication tables), so 560 ÷ 7 = 80. So each pile will have 80 beads in it.

2. 650 mm
The length of beads will be 50 × 13 mm. 100 × 13 mm = 1300 mm. So 50 × 13 mm = 1300 mm ÷ 2 = 650 mm.

3. 5
5 of the 9 cubes have exactly 2 spotted faces, as shown:

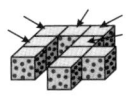

4. (4, 5)
The reflected shape will look like this:
So the new coordinates of the labelled corner are (4, 5).

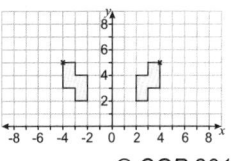

5.   B
$1/4$ of the girls and $1/4$ of the boys got 5 stars.
$36 \div 4 = 9$ girls got 5 stars. $28 \div 4 = 7$ boys got 5 stars, so 2 more girls than boys got 5 stars. So option B is true, and this also shows that option A is false. Option C is false because the amounts less than 5 stars take up three quarters of the pie, which is 75%, not 70%. The number of children with 5 stars is $9 + 7 = 16$. So option E is false. The total number of children is $36 + 28 = 64$. 16 is not half of 64, so option D is false.

6.   7
70° of the pie chart represents girls who got 3 stars. Each girl is represented by $360° \div 36 = 10°$. So 70° must represent $70 \div 10 = 7$ girls. Half of the boys got 3 stars; $28 \div 2 = 14$. So $14 - 7 = 7$ more boys than girls earned exactly 3 stars.

7.   C
The length of one side of an octagon is $24 \text{ cm} \div 8 = 3 \text{ cm}$. The sides of the octagons and squares are the same length. The shaded region has 16 sides. So the perimeter is $16 \times 3 = 48$ cm.

8.   7 and 17
Find the prime numbers between 1 and 20: 2, 3, 5, 7, 11, 13, 17, 19. Add up any pairs which have a difference of 10: $3 + 13 = 16$. $7 + 17 = 24$. So Connie is thinking of 7 and 17.

9.   23%
2 litres = 2000 ml. Dulcie has drunk $460/2000$ of her target water total. Simplify the fraction by dividing the top and bottom by 20 so that the denominator is 100: $23/100$. So she has drunk 23% of her target water volume.

10.   B
Round 290 ml up to 300 ml and estimate the number of glasses needed.
6 glasses × 300 ml = 1800 ml, so 6 glasses won't be enough. 7 glasses × 300 ml = 2100 ml.
Use partitioning to work out that $7 \times 290 = 2030$ ml. So she needs at least 7 glasses to meet her total.

11.   0.265 kg
The teddy and the car weigh $894 \text{ g} \div 2 = 447$ g. So the teddy weighs $447 \text{ g} - 182 \text{ g} = 265$ g. Divide by 1000 to convert to kg: $265 \div 1000 = 0.265$ kg.

12.   B
$2(x^2 - 14) = 44$. Divide both sides of the equation by 2 to give $x^2 - 14 = 22$.
Add 14 to both sides to give $x^2 = 36$.
$6^2 = 36$. So Manoj is thinking of the number 6.

Puzzles 5 — page 81
Percy's Picture Puzzle

Test 26 — pages 82-84
1.   £704 305.08
Seven hundred and four thousand pounds is £704 000. Three hundred and five pounds is £305. Eight pence is £0.08. Adding these together gives £704 305.08.

2.   29
You find each term by adding 3 to the previous term. So the next terms will be 17, 20, 23, 26, 29, ... The 10th term is 29.

3.   24
One quarter of the people are vegetarian, so there must be $6 \times 4 = 24$ people coming in total.

4.   E
The total number of books is $3 + 7 + 5 + 2 + 1 = 18$. The total number of books that are fantasy or sci-fi is $7 + 5 = 12$. So $12/18$ books are fantasy or sci-fi. Simplify the fraction by dividing the numerator and denominator by 6: $12/18 = 2/3$.

5.   B
Area of a square = length × length, so the length of one side multiplied by itself equals 9.
So the length of one side = 3 cm ($9 = 3 \times 3$).
So the perimeter of the square is $3 + 3 + 3 + 3 = 12$ cm.

6.   C
Angles in a triangle add to 180°. Angles in an equilateral triangle are equal so each angle is $180 \div 3 = 60°$. Angles on a straight line add to 180°, so angle z is $180 - 60 = 120°$.

7.   0
The shape does not have any lines of symmetry.

8.   D
The area of the rectangle is $3 \times 6 = 18$ units^2. The area of one triangle is $1/2 \times 3 \times 2 = 3$ units^2. The total area of 3 triangles is $3 \times 3 = 9$ units^2. This is different to the area of the rectangle, so D is false.

9.   C
The smallest possible width of the oven is 75.5 cm (anything lower than 5 in the tenths column would round down to 75 cm). The smallest possible width of the space is 77.45 cm (anything lower than 5 in the hundredths column would round down to 77.4 cm). So C is the correct option.

10.   £72.00
One ball of wool costs £2.60, so half a ball costs £2.60 ÷ 2 = £1.30. 1 scarf needs 1.5 balls of wool, which costs £2.60 + £1.30 = £3.90. The wool for 30 scarves costs £3.90 × 30 = £117 (use partitioning or the column method). To find the profit, subtract the cost of the wool to make 30 scarves from the total amount made from selling the scarves: £189 − £117 = £72.

11.   E
Each friend gets £150 ÷ 7. Using long division: Rounding down, gives 21.42 to the nearest penny.

```
       21.42 r 6p
     7)150.00
       140.00
        10.00
         7.00
         3.00
         2.80
         0.20
         0.14
         0.06
```

12. 16
Use knowledge of the order of operations to work out
5 + 4 × 3: First do the multiplication: 4 × 3 = 12.
Then do the addition: 12 + 5 = 17.
$n < 5 + 4 × 3$ means that n is less than 5 + 4 × 3, so
$n < 17$. The largest square number below 17 is 16 (4^2).
So the largest number n could be is 16.

Test 27 — pages 85-87

1. S
270° is 3 lots of 90° (using multiplication
tables knowledge: 3 × 9 = 27).
So the arrow will move 3 right-angles
around the weather vane and point south.

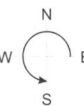

2. 5
The mean = total age ÷ number of cousins.
So the number of cousins = total age ÷ mean.
So Mike has 40 ÷ 8 = 5 cousins.

3. E
Grams and kilograms are units of mass, and millimetres
are units of length. So that rules out options A, B and D.
A volume of 2.5 millilitres is very small (option C), so the
units are most likely to be litres (option E).

4. £1.00
$^1/_3$ of twelve 20 pence pieces is 12 ÷ 3 = 4. So she gives
her nephew 4 × 20p = 80p in 20 pence pieces.
$^1/_4$ of eight 10 pence pieces is 8 ÷ 4 = 2. So she gives
her nephew 2 × 10p = 20p in 10 pence pieces.
So in total Dora gives 80p + 20p = 100p = £1.00.

5. 3
Find all of the factors of 60: 1, 2, 3, 4, 5, 6, 10, 12, 15,
20, 30, 60. A prime number has exactly 2 factors:
1 and itself. Find the numbers in the list which are prime
numbers: 2, 3, 5. So there are 3 prime numbers that are
factors of 60.

6. E
Convert the fractions so they have a common
denominator. $3^3/_4 = 3^{15}/_{20}$. $^1/_5 = ^4/_{20}$. So Lola has
$3^{15}/_{20} - ^4/_{20} = 3^{11}/_{20}$ packs of chocolate buttons left.

7. 20
Each pentagon symbol in the pictogram shows 25 trees,
so each triangle that makes up the symbol is worth
25 ÷ 5 = 5 trees. There are 4 more triangles for ash
trees than elm trees. So there are 4 × 5 = 20 more ash
trees than elm trees.

8. D
Add up the total number of triangle symbols for
each tree: 13 (ash) + 9 (elm) + 8 (fir) + 10 (oak) = 40.
So $^8/_{40}$ of the triangles are for fir trees.
Simplify this fraction by dividing the numerator and
denominator by 8: $^1/_5$.

9. E
A regular shape has sides of equal length. So the
perimeter = the length of one side × the number of sides
= 5 cm × x = $5x$ cm (option E).

10. 360
60 cm = 600 mm. 36 cm = 360 mm. 45 cm = 450 mm.
Work out how many 15 mm fit in 600 mm:
60 ÷ 15 = 4, so 600 ÷ 15 = 40. So 40 books can fit in
one row along the length of the box. Work out how many
120 mm fit in 360 mm width: 36 ÷ 12 = 3, so
360 ÷ 120 = 3. So 3 rows of books can fit in the
bottom of the box. Work out how many 150 mm fit in
450 mm height: 45 ÷ 15 = 3, so 450 ÷ 150 = 3.
So 3 layers of books will fill up the height of the box.
One layer of books will have 40 × 3 = 120 books.
So the whole box will contain 120 × 3 = 360 books.

11. 120
Work out how many boxes will be completely full.
360 + 360 = 720 (2 boxes). 720 + 360 = 1080
(3 boxes). 1080 + 360 = 1440 (4 boxes). There are
not enough books to fill 4 boxes, so there will be 3 full
boxes and 1200 – 1080 = 120 books left over.

12. D
Find the value of n by using $5 = ^1/_2(n + 1)$.
If $^1/_2$ of $(n + 1)$ is 5, then $(n + 1)$ must be 2 × 5 = 10.
So, 10 = n + 1. Subtract 1 from both sides to get:
9 = n. So the 9th term (option D) in the sequence is 5.

Test 28 — pages 88-90

1. 1400
7 × 200 = 7 × 2 × 100 = 14 × 100 = 1400.

2. £33.65
Noah needs to save £50.00 – £16.35 = £33.65 more
(use partitioning).

3. £12.50
25% is the same as one quarter, so find 25% of £50 by
dividing it by 4, which is the same as halving it twice:
£50 ÷ 2 = £25. £25 ÷ 2 = £12.50.
So 25% of £50 is £12.50.

4. 9 cm
Count the total number of sides of all four shapes =
3 + 4 + 5 + 6 = 18 sides. Multiply this by 2 to get
the total perimeter of all four shapes: 18 × 2 = 36 cm.
Divide the total perimeter by 4 (the number of shapes)
to find the mean perimeter: 36 ÷ 4 = 9 cm.

5. D
Twice as many guests chose eggs as chose pastries, so
option B is incorrect. Twice as many guests chose cereal
as chose fruit, so options A and E are incorrect. Nine
times as many guests chose cereal as chose pastries, so
C is incorrect. D must be the correct list.

6. 27°
Parallelograms have 2 pairs of equal opposite angles.
So the bottom right angle of the parallelogram must also
equal 63°. Angles on a straight line add to 180° so
angle a = 180 – 63 – 90 = 27°.

7. £5.50
Belle buys the same as Amy plus one coffee, so one
coffee costs £6.25 – £4.50 = £1.75.
So one cake costs £4.50 – £1.75 = £2.75.
So two cakes cost 2 × £2.75 = £5.50.

8. A
Adbul has $^1/_3$ of a melon. $^1/_3 ÷ 4 = ^1/_{3 × 4} = ^1/_{12}$.

9.   0.06 s
The winner is the swimmer with the shortest time. This is Kim with 29.98 s. The person in second place is Li with 30.04 s. Kim is 30.04 − 29.98 seconds faster than Li. Find the difference by counting up: from 29.98 to 30 is 0.02. From 30 to 30.04 is 0.04. So 30.04 − 29.98 = 0.02 + 0.04 = 0.06 s.

10.   D
Parallelograms have two pairs of equal parallel sides. So find pairs of points that join to form parallel lines and are the same distance apart.
So B, C, E and F are the vertices of the parallelogram.

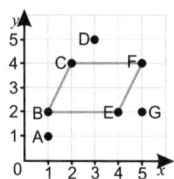

11.   1.5 cm²
The area of a parallelogram = base × height. The base of the parallelogram is 3 grid squares = 3 × 0.5 = 1.5 cm. The height of the parallelogram is 2 grid squares = 2 × 0.5 = 1 cm. So area = 1.5 × 1 = 1.5 cm².

12.   90 mins
Ollie could walk w miles in one hour, so to walk $3/4 w$ miles to the bakery, it would take $3/4$ of an hour = 45 minutes. So to go to the bakery and back, it would take 45 × 2 = 90 mins.

Test 29 — pages 91-93

1.   120 g
Sally gets 360 g ÷ 3.
36 ÷ 3 = 12, so 360 ÷ 3 = 120 g.

2.   30%
Work out the total number of half segments that have been shaded: 4 + 3 + 2 = 9.
Each star can be divided into 10 half segments, so there are 10 × 3 = 30 half segments in total. So $9/30$ half segments have been shaded. Simplify this fraction by dividing the numerator and denominator by 3: $3/10$. This is equivalent to 30%.

3.   8 cm
The total perimeter of three stars is 240 cm. Each star has 10 sides, so there are 10 × 3 = 30 sides in total. So the length of one side is 240 ÷ 30 = 8 cm (use 24 ÷ 3 = 8).

4.   B
3.58 is 100 times smaller than 358.
So 1 690 834 ÷ 3.58 will be 100 times bigger than 1 690 834 ÷ 358.
So the answer is 4723 × 100 = 472 300

5.   7 cm
The rectangle is made from 2 equal triangles, so the rectangle's area is twice the area of one triangle = 14 cm² × 2 = 28 cm².
Area of a rectangle = length × width, so 28 = 4 × width. So the width must be 28 ÷ 4 = 7 cm.

6.   8192
Number of bits in a kilobyte = number of bits in a byte × number of bytes in a kilobyte:

```
    1024
 ×     8
    8192
     13
```

7.   C
As a fraction of the whole circle, $144/360$ children said No. Simplify the fraction by dividing the numerator and the denominator by 12: $12/30$, and then again by dividing the numerator and denominator by 6: $2/5$.
$2/5$ is equivalent to 40% (option C).

8.   6
40% of the class said No (from previous answer), so 100 − 40 = 60% said Yes.
40% = 12 people. 10% = 12 ÷ 4 = 3. So 60% of the class is 3 × 6 = 18 people. This is 18 − 12 = 6 more than the number of people who said No.

9.   C
First work out the value of $2/3$ of £72. $1/3$ of £72 = 72 ÷ 3 = £24 (use short division). So $2/3$ of £72 is 24 × 2 = £48. Next work out double the amount of £22.50: 22.50 × 2 = £45. Ella has between £45 and £48. So she could have £46.50 (option C).

10.   D
Work out which corner joins to corner M:

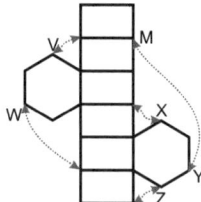

So corner M joins to corner Y.

11.   17 150
Work out 1% of 49 000: 49 000 ÷ 100 = 490.
Work out 35% of 49 000 by multiplying 490 by 35:

```
      490
 ×     35
     2450
         4
 + 14700
       2
    17150
        1
```

12.   B
The mass of the bowl is 90 g. The mass of the flour is 10 × f = 10f g. So the combined mass is 10f + 90.

Test 30 — pages 94-96

1.   2
8 more than −8 is 0, so 10 more is an extra 2.

2.   1.1 kg
The apples weigh 700g ÷ 1000 = 0.7 kg.
So the grapes must weigh 1.8 − 0.7 = 1.1 kg.

3.   119 g
The remaining 5 apples have a mass of 700 g − 105 g = 595 g.
So their mean mass is 595 ÷ 5.
Use short division: 5)595 So the mean is 119 g.

4.   £6.79
To get 14 litres of milk, he buys 14 ÷ 2 = 7 containers. This costs 7 × 97p. 97p = £1 − 3p, so 7 × 97p = (7 × £1) −(7 × 3p) = £7 − 21p = £6.79.

5. 49 cm²
The length of one side of the square is the same as the length of one side of the pentagon. Work out the length of one side of the pentagon by dividing the perimeter by 5: 35 ÷ 5 = 7 cm. The area of the square is length × width = 7 × 7 = 49 cm².

6. 7
Tuesday was the busiest day this year, with 10 children, and Thursday was the least busy day last year, with 3 children. 10 − 3 = 7.

7. E
This year there were 5 + 10 + 3 + 4 + 8 = 30 children in total. Last year there were 9 + 8 + 6 + 3 + 5 = 31 children in total. There were fewer children this year than last year, so statement E is not true.

8. D
First take off the extra 10 pigs. 58 − 10 = 48. This number of animals is made up of an equal number of cows and pigs. So there are 48 ÷ 2 = 24 of each. Adding the extra 10 pigs on gives 24 + 10 = 34 pigs (option D).

9. 36
The new number of pigs = 34 × 2 = 68. The old number of cows was 34 − 10 = 24. $1/3$ of 24 = 24 ÷ 3 = 8, so the new number of cows is 24 + 8 = 32. So there are now 68 − 32 = 36 more pigs than cows.

10. 35°
The angles around a point add up to 360°.
So $a + 2a + 165° + 90° = 360°$.
This means that $3a + 255° = 360°$, and so $3a = 105°$.
So a must be 105° ÷ 3 = 35°.

11. B
The reduced prices for each option are as follows:
A: 10% of £2000 = £2000 ÷ 10 = £200, so 30% of £2000 = 3 × £200 = £600. So the reduced price is £2000 − £600 = £1400. B: 25% of £1800 = £1800 ÷ 4 = £450. So the reduced price is £1800 − £450 = £1350. C: £1600 − £150 = £1450.
D: $1/3$ of £2100 = £2100 ÷ 3 = £700. So the reduced price is £2100 − £700 = £1400.
E: £1500 − £80 = £1420.
So B is the cheapest, at £1350.

12. D
For the other two sets of coordinates, the x-coordinate has increased by 3, and the y-coordinate has decreased by 2. So (x, y) will be translated to $(x + 3, y − 2)$.

Test 31 — pages 97-99
1. £0.65
1 kg = 1000 g. 1000 g costs £6.50, so 100 g costs £6.50 ÷ 10 = £0.65.

2. C
The time where the temperature reaches 0 °C is the point where the line crosses the x-axis. Each division on the axis represents 1 minute. The line crosses the x-axis 4.5 divisions after 5 minutes, which is 5 + 4.5 = 9.5 mins = 9 mins 30 secs.

3. 10 °C
At 0 minutes, the temperature is about 5.5 °C.
At 16 minutes, the temperature is about −4.5 °C.

Find the difference between 5.5 °C and −4.5 °C:
5.5 to 0 = 5.5. 0 to −4.5 = 4.5 °C.
Difference = 5.5 + 4.5 = 10 °C

4. 4 cm
The volume of the cube = length × width × height = 2 × 2 × 2 = 8 cm³. So the volume of the cuboid is also 8 cm³.
So the height of the cuboid = volume ÷ (length × width) = 8 ÷ (2 × 1) = 8 ÷ 2 = 4 cm.

5. D
Write down the terms in the sequence by dividing the previous term by 2 until you reach a number that is not whole: 32, 16, 8, 4, 2, 1, 0.5. So the 7th term in the sequence is the first that is not a whole number.

6. 303 mm
Find the total length of the candles: 38 × 6 = 228 mm (use partitioning). Find the total length of the spaces between the candles: 15 × 5 = 75 mm. So the shelf is 228 + 75 = 303 mm

7. 45
10% of 300 bouquets = 30 bouquets.
So, 20% = 2 × 30 = 60 pink bouquets. 60% = 6 × 30 = 180 red bouquets. So there are 300 − 60 − 180 − 15 = 45 yellow bouquets.

8. 900
From the previous answer, there are 60 pink bouquets. So there are 60 × 12 = 720 pink roses.
There are 15 × 12 = 180 white roses (use partitioning). So total pink and white roses = 720 + 180 = 900.

9. E
In Roman numerals, D is 500, C is 100, L is 50, X is 10, V is 5 and I is 1. 600 is 100 more than 500 (DC), 80 is 3 tens more than 50 (LXXX), and an extra 5 gives DCLXXXV.

10. C
36.6% is the same as 36.6 ÷ 100 = 0.366, not 3.66.

11. 42 cm²
Each triangle has a base of 14 ÷ 2 = 7 cm, and a height of 6 ÷ 2 = 3 cm. Area of a triangle = $1/2$ × base × height, so each triangle has an area of $1/2$ × 7 × 3 = 10.5 cm².
So the four triangles have a total area of:
4 × 10.5 = 42 cm² (use partitioning).

12. D
If the mean is m, then the total of the numbers must be $3m$. The only set of numbers that adds up to $3m$ is option D: $m − 5 + m + 2 + m + 3 = 3m$.

Puzzles 6 — page 100
Funny Money
The bank should give Daisy 15 horns (£97.50) and 1 flower (£2.50).

Painting by Numbers

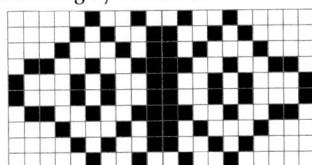

Gently does it... Please remove this Answer Book carefully to keep your books in perfect condition!